Eat n SHUT UP

ITALIAN RECIPES ROOTED IN TRADITION

Maria Caporaso Magdalen

www.eatnshutup.com

Mangia é Statti Zitto!

Eat N Shut Up
Italian Recipes Rooted in Tradition

Maria Caporaso Magdalen

Copyright © 2025
First Edition

@eatnshutup

Softcover ISBN: 979-8-218-70277-9
Hardcover ISBN: 979-8-218-71755-1

All rights reserved under International and
Pan-American Copyright Conventions. Manufactured in USA.

No part of this book may be reproduced, stored, or transmitted in any form or by any means—electronic, mechanical, photocopying, recording, or otherwise—without prior written permission from the publisher or author, except for brief quotations in reviews or educational purposes.

Cover & Book Design: Kristy Twellmann • umbrellasquared.com
Cover & Food Photography: Ken Hild Photography
Hair & Makeup: LisaMarie Glick • www.misslisamarie.com • @M1ssL1saMar1e

www.eatnshutup.com

Dedication

This book is dedicated to my Grandparents and parents.
Thank you for filling our home with the rich flavors of our heritage and the warmth of your love. Every simmering pot, every hand rolled pasta and every shared meal taught me more than just recipes, it taught me the value of family, tradition, and joy in the simple moments. Your stories, your laughter and your dedication to preserving our Italian roots shaped me in ways I'll cherish forever. This book is a tribute to your legacy, a celebration of food that brought us together, and a promise to keep those traditions alive. Though time may pass, the love and lessons you've given me will always season my life.

Grazie per tutto
Con tutto il mio cuore

Thank you for everything! With all my heart!

Maria

Contents

MEET MARIA 1
BACK TO BASICS 5

DRINKS
Espresso Martini 9
Limoncello 11
Zabaglione 13

SOUPS
Clam Chowder 17
Cream of Asparagus Soup 19
Creamy Broccoli Soup 21
Creamy Potato Soup 23
Escarole & Beans with Sausage & Orecchiette 25
Italian Wedding Soup 27
Lentil Soup 29
Pasta Fagioli 31
Roasted Butternut Squash Soup 33

APPETIZERS
Burrata with Roasted Tomatoes & Garlic 37
Calamari Oreganata 39
Easter Pie 39
Eggplant Rollatini 43
Fried Burrata Bombs 45
Mozzarella in Carrozza 47
Pan Seared Scallops 49
Scallops Saltimbocca 51
Sicilian Style Stuffed Peppers 53
Spinach Artichoke Dip 55

Stuffed & Fried Sicilian Olives 57
Stuffed Cherry Peppers 59
Stuffed Meatballs 61
Stuffed Mushrooms 63
Stuffed Peppers & Rice 65

SIDES
Arancini 69
Asparagus with Béchamel Sauce 71
Polenta 73
Red, White and Blue Potatoes 75
Risotto 77
Sauteed Cabbage with Pancetta 79
Stuffed Artichokes 81
Stuffed Cabbage 83
Suppli 85

PASTA
Aunt Concetta's Manicotti 89
Broccoli Rabe with Sausage & Orecchiette 91
Calamarata Pasta with Italian Tuna
    & Tomato Sauce 93
Gnocchi 95
Gnudi 97
Lasagna 99
Linguine & Clams 101

Lobster & Shrimp Fra Diavolo 103
Pasta alla Norma 105
Penne alla Vodka 107
Puttanesca 109
Quick Marinara Sauce 111
Spaghetti Aglio e'Alici 113
Spaghetti Carbonara 115

MEAT/CARNE DISHES

Braciole 119
Chicken Cacciatore 121
Chicken Meatballs 123
Chicken Piccata 125
Easy Whole Roasted Chicken 127
Pork Chops with Cherry Peppers 129
Sausage with Onions, Fennel & Grapes 131
Steak Pizzaiola 133
Stuffed Chicken Cutlets 135
Tripe 137

FISH/PESCARE

Baked Clams 141
Bronzino 143
Cod Puttanesca 145
Grilled Polpo 147
Insalata di Mare 149
Mussels Marinara 151

Shrimp Oreganata 153
Stuffed Calamari 155
Stuffed Flounder 157

DESSERTS

Italian Cheesecake 161
Grain Pie 163
Italian Rainbow Cookies 165
Lemon Ricotta Cake 167
Pignoli Cookies 169
Rice Pudding 171
Sicilian Orange Cake 173
Tiramisu 175

ITALIAN/AMERICAN WORDS & PHRASES 177
ACKNOWLEDGMENTS 179
INDEX 181

Meet Maria

I CAN STILL HEAR THEIR VOICES.

I can still remember the delicious smells that drifted from next door. The memories are etched in my mind—my grandfather walking me hand-in-hand to the bus stop, whistling softly as he came by each morning with fresh eggs and bread. Growing up next to my grandparents was one of the greatest gifts of my early years, and those moments laid the foundation for who I am today.

I'm the youngest in my family, with three older, amazing brothers and loving, hardworking parents. While my parents devoted themselves to running a limousine business, I spent much of my time with my grandparents. Looking back now, those were the golden days—the ones filled with laughter, love, and the comfort of daily life in the kitchen and garden.

Both of my grandfathers had incredible gardens. You could truly eat off the land. And as fate would have it, they both came from the same town in Naples—Avellino. My maternal Grandmother is from Agrigento, Sicily and paternal Grandmother from Calabria. I feel truly blessed to have learned so many recipes from both the North and South of Italy. It's no surprise that food became such a strong part of my identity.

My love for cooking didn't come from formal lessons, but from simply being beside them—watching, learning, tasting, and creating. It was in those everyday moments that my passion was born. I was fortunate to come from generations of incredible cooks. Aside from my grandparents, I learned from my parents, Aunts, and brothers who each brought their own talents into the kitchen.

Traditions have always been at the heart of our family. Sunday dinners meant meatballs, braciole, sausage, and some form of macaroni but not before going to Sunday mass. My Italian American family was deeply rooted in faith and religion, which I instill in my five children today. Going to Sunday mass and religious holidays were a given. Often times my parents would invite priests to join us for Sunday dinner. Aside from being a full time preschool teacher, I have also taught religion for the past 20 years at Saint Joseph's just as my mom did. Faith and food seem to go hand and hand in my family. Holidays were—and still are—a celebration of togetherness through food. Some of my most cherished traditions include Thanksgiving with

stuffed artichokes, Christmas Eve with the Seven Fishes, and Easter with pizza rustica and Easter bread. These are the flavors of my childhood, and the memories I hold most dear.

As the years go on, I make it a point to keep these traditions alive—for my family, and for the generations to come. Hosting holidays, birthdays and any form of celebration has always brought me joy. My husband and I are both the youngest in our families, which meant we had a whole crew of nieces and nephews long before we had kids of our own. I absolutely loved having them over for sleepovers—turning the simplest meals into something fun and memorable. Whether it was themed breakfasts, homemade pizza nights, or baking cookies together, I've always found joy in making people feel at home and well-fed.

Being a mom of my five children is a wild, beautiful, chaotic and the most deeply rewarding job of my life. It is filled with endless love, laughter, food and laundry. So. Much. Laundry. Nothing beats the joy of watching my children Rosalie, Gianni, Sophia, Lucia and Maria truly enjoy a meal I made with love. I feel I am sharing my past with them through my cooking. It is truly something special when I have all five in the kitchen with me—creating new memories, hearing about their day, while also reminiscing about when they were all little. One of my favorite stories is from my daughter Rosalie's second Christmas Eve at my father's house, when she happily ate her way through all of the Seven Fishes! Moments like that remind me how powerful food can be in shaping childhood memories.

To every parent reading this: I encourage you to introduce your children to new recipes and expand their palates early on. In today's world, where taking a family of seven out to a nice restaurant isn't always practical, I've learned to recreate restaurant-quality meals at home, on a budget. With a little creativity and love, you can give your family a five-star experience right at your own kitchen table.

This cookbook is a love letter to my memories, my roots, and to the joy that comes from feeding the people I love.

As my Grandfather Modestino said daily, Mangia e'Statti Zitto!

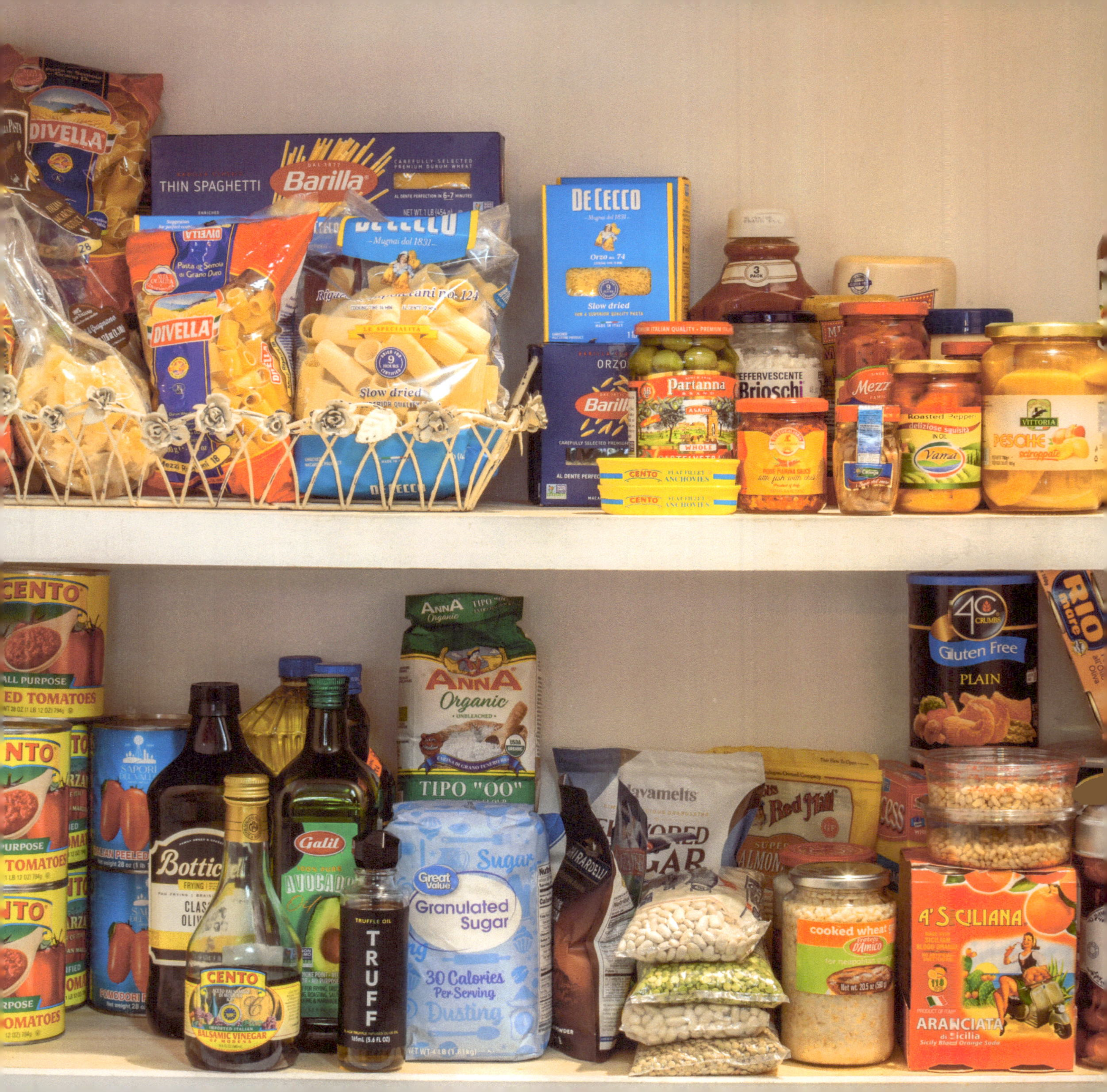
DIVELLA
THIN SPAGHETTI
Barilla
DE CECCO
Mugnai dal 1831
Slow dried
ORZO
Partanna
EFFERVESCENTE
Brioschi
CENTO
FLAT FILLET ANCHOVIES
Roasted Peppers
VITTORIA
PESCHE
ALL PURPOSE
TOMATOES
ANNA
Organic
TIPO "OO"
Gluten Free
PLAIN
Galil
Great Value
Granulated Sugar
30 Calories Per Serving
TRUFFLE OIL
TRUFF
BALSAMIC VINEGAR
cooked wheat
A'SICILIANA
ARANCIATA
di Sicilia
Sicily Blood Orange Soda

Back to Basics

Having a well stocked pantry makes all the difference when it comes to making easy meals, quick and stress free dinners or for those unexpected nights when company comes over and you need to quickly throw together a meal. **A solid foundation of pantry staples should include...**

- **Grains:** rice and an assortment of pastas
- **Legumes:** a nice variety of bagged beans for hearty soups
- **Canned Goods:** beans, vegetables and most definitely tomatoes
- **Oil/Vinegar:** red wine vinegar & balsamic, vegetable, truffle, avocado and of course extra virgin olive oil
- **Baking Staples:** sugar, all purpose flour, gluten free flour and Napoletana Tipo 00 Flour
- **Condiments:** mayo, ketchup, mustard
- **Nuts:** pignoli, pistachio and your personal favorites
- **Spices/Dried Herbs:** salt, pepper, sea and kosher salt, parsley, basil, thyme, oregano and rosemary

This well stocked pantry will help provide peace of mind ensuring you will always be ready to whip up something delicious in no time. You will have the confidence to cook like a boss any night of the week.

DRINKS

ESPRESSO MARTINI

 MAKES ONE

INGREDIENTS

2 oz Vodka
2 oz Freshly Brewed Espresso
2 oz Kahlúa
½ oz Simple Syrup
Shaker
2 Cups Ice
1 Chilled Martini Glass
3 Coffee Beans

DIRECTIONS

1. Start by brewing your espresso with your preferred method.
2. Let cool completely.
3. Place shaker in refrigerator while espresso cools.
4. Add ice to the shaker before adding espresso, vodka, Kahlua and simple syrup.
5. Shake well and serve in a chilled glass.
6. Garnish with a few coffee beans.

Pro Tip: *I prefer Van Gogh Double Espresso vodka.*

Mangia é Statti Zitto!

LIMONCELLO

 MAKES 48OZ

Limoncello is an Italian lemon liqueur. The oils from the marinated lemon peels give the intense lemon flavor. It is delicious and refreshing. Limoncello is also known to help with digestion.

INGREDIENTS

11 Large Lemons
2 ¼ Cups Vodka
6 Cups Water
2 ½ Cups Sugar

DIRECTIONS

1. Wash and soak lemons for 5 minutes and dry well.
2. Peel lemons carefully making sure to only remove the yellow layer.
3. Place lemon peels in a sealed jar with the vodka.
4. Place in a cool dry place for 20-30 days.
5. Place the water and sugar in a saucepan and bring to a boil.
6. Mix for 6-8 minutes or until sugar is completely dissolved.
7. Place strainer over pot and carefully pour the vodka over the strainer into the pot.
8. Store in refrigerator in an airtight container.
9. Serve in chilled glasses.

Mangia é Statti Zitto!

ZABAGLIONE

 SERVES 3-4

This was made for me by a family friend and grew to become a special treat I give to my family on occasion. A delicious twist on your typical morning shot of espresso. A lot of people would compare this to an Italian eggnog.

INGREDIENTS

4 Shots (8 oz) Espresso
4 Eggs
4 Heaping Tbs of Sugar
Double Broiler (optional)

DIRECTIONS

1. Prepare the espresso with your preferred method and set aside.
2. Bring water to a low boil in either a double broiler or saucepan.
3. Over a double broiler, place egg yolks and sugar.
4. If you do not have a double broiler, a glass bowl sitting in a saucepan of water works well.
5. Whisk until you get a custard-like consistency.
6. Slowly add the espresso to the egg custard while whisking.
7. Whisk until light brown and creamy.
8. Serve in 3-4 individual espresso cups.

Mangia é Statti Zitto!

SOUPS

CLAM CHOWDER

SERVES 8-10

This creamy, cozy chowder is perfection! It is seafood bliss made simple.

INGREDIENTS

3 Dozen Clams
32 oz Vegetable Broth
1 Cup White Wine
2 Cups Bacon
1 Large Onion
3 Stalks of Celery
4 Garlic Cloves
3-4 Potatoes
2 Cups Heavy Cream
Salt
Pepper
Parsley for Garnish

DIRECTIONS

1. Using a brush or cloth give the clams a good scrub.
2. Place clams in a deep skillet on medium-low heat with white wine and just enough broth to cover the clams.
3. Remove them from the pan as soon as they pop open. If you keep them in too long they will overcook and become rubbery.
4. Let them cool before removing from the shells and place in the food processor.
5. In a large pot, brown the bacon until crispy and remove using a slotted spoon.
6. Keep the bacon grease in the pot and add chopped onion, chopped celery and chopped garlic.
7. Season with pepper.
8. Sauté until soft, then add to the food processor with the clams.
9. Pulse until chopped a little at a time. You don't want to make a paste, so pulse slowly.
10. Afterwards, transfer the clam mixture to a bowl.
11. Add butter and chopped potatoes to a separate pot on medium heat. I like to use Yukon Gold or red potatoes.
12. Season with salt and pepper.
13. Add the rest of the broth and cook potatoes until the fork goes in with ease.
14. Transfer potatoes to the food processor and pulse until smooth.
15. Add everything back to the pot with the heavy cream and season to taste.
16. Stir and keep on low simmer for 15 mins.
17. Ladle soup into deep bowls and top with chopped bacon and fresh parsley.

Mangia é Statti Zitto!

CREAM OF ASPARAGUS SOUP

 SERVES 8-10

This is my personal favorite soup recipe. Asparagus is so healthy for you. It's chock full of antioxidants and Vitamin K. Healthy Meets Heavenly!

INGREDIENTS

- 4 Bunches Asparagus
- 3-4 Garlic Cloves
- 1-2 Large Onions
- ½ Stick or 4 Tbs Butter
- 32 oz Chicken or Vegetable Broth
- 3 Cups Heavy Cream
- 6 Cups Water
- Pinch Of Nutmeg
- Goat Cheese
  (Teaspoon per serving)
- Salt and Pepper to taste
- Extra Virgin Olive Oil

DIRECTIONS

1. Wash the asparagus before starting.
2. Add extra virgin olive oil to a pot along with ½ a stick of butter.
3. Add 1-2 diced onions and sauté.
4. Add 3-4 chopped cloves of garlic and 4 big bunches of asparagus chopped small.
5. Season with salt and pepper and sauté 10-12 minutes.
6. Once the veggies are tender, add the broth and water.
7. Bring to a boil and cook for an additional 7-8 minutes.
8. Using a slotted spoon, remove asparagus from the pot and place in a blender, blending on medium speed until puréed.
9. Pour back into the pot with the broth and cook on low heat.
10. Add heavy cream and simmer on low for 10 minutes.
11. To thicken, remove one ladle of soup and place in a glass bowl.
12. Add one tablespoon of flour, whisking until the flour is well incorporated and pour back into the pot.
13. Serve this delicious creamy soup in a nice sized bowl.
14. Add a teaspoon of goat cheese in the center of the bowl with a pinch of nutmeg.
15. Place one small asparagus in the middle for garnish and enjoy.

Mangia é Statti Zitto!

CREAMY BROCCOLI SOUP

 SERVES 6-8

Creamy Broccoli Soup is full of vitamins and antioxidants. This is a great way to get vegetables into your body. Don't mind the bacon as it adds a little salty flavor with some crispy texture. Perfect for a rainy day!

INGREDIENTS

4 Heads of Broccoli

3 Large Red Potatoes with skin on

1 Container Of Chicken Broth (about 4 Cups)

6 Cups of Water

½ Cup of Bacon (chopped)

2 Cups of Light or Heavy Cream

Salt

Pepper

Shredded Cheddar

DIRECTIONS

1. Cut about ½ cup of bacon.
2. Fry in a large pot until crispy.
3. Remove bacon from the pot using a slotted spoon and set aside.
4. Leave bacon oil in the pan and add in 1 chopped onion.
5. Cut up broccoli and red potatoes (leave the skin on) and add to the pot. Season with salt.
6. Pour in chicken broth (you can use low sodium chicken broth if you prefer).
7. To the broth, add the water and bring to a boil.
8. Once the potatoes are fork tender, remove the broccoli and potatoes from the pot and place in a blender. You might need to blend in batches if it doesn't all fit at first.
9. Once you have a smoothie-like consistency, pour the soup back into the pot and add 2 cups of cream.
10. Stir and simmer on low for 10-12 minutes.
11. Serve with shredded cheddar and a few pieces of that chopped bacon.

Mangia é Statti Zitto!

CREAMY POTATO SOUP

 SERVES 6-8

Creamy Potato Soup is the ultimate comfort food that is like giving your stomach a hug.

INGREDIENTS

- 5 Idaho Potatoes
- 3 Large Red Potatoes
- 4 oz Chopped Bacon
- 1 Large Onion
- 32 oz Container Of Chicken Broth
- 32 oz Heavy Cream
- 2 Cups Cheddar Cheese (shredded)
- 1 Bunch Scallions
- 6 oz Sour Cream
- Nutmeg
- Kosher Salt
- Black Pepper

DIRECTIONS

1. Cut your bacon into bite size pieces and fry them in a large pot until crispy.
2. Remove using a slotted spoon, leaving bacon oils in the pot and set aside.
3. Add diced onion to the pot and sauté on low heat until translucent.
4. Peel and cut Idaho potatoes to add to the pot.
5. Add red potatoes to the pot leaving the skin on.
6. Season with a pinch of Kosher salt and pepper.
7. Pour in chicken broth and heavy cream.
8. Bring to a boil and then keep on low heat for 20 minutes. Once the potatoes are done, you should be able to easily insert a fork into the potatoes.
9. Using a slotted spoon, take out potatoes and add them to a blender, leaving the liquid in the pot on low heat.
10. Blend the potatoes until creamy and pour back into the pot.
11. Add a pinch of nutmeg and stir for a few minutes.
12. Garnish each bowl with diced scallions, sour cream, bacon bits and shredded cheese.

Mangia é Statti Zitto!

ESCAROLE & BEANS WITH SAUSAGE & ORECCHIETTE

 SERVES 8-10

This dish is such a classic and was a staple growing up. My grandparents made this often and it was always served with warm bread right out of the oven. Many Italian Americans call this dish "Ska-role" n beans.

INGREDIENTS

- 2 Bunches Escarole
- 2 Pounds Sausage
- 4 Garlic Cloves
- 1 Qt Chicken Broth
- 1 Pound Canned Cannellini Beans
- ½ Pound Orecchiette (optional) Pasta
- Red Pepper Flakes
- Extra Virgin Olive Oil
- Salt
- Pecorino Romano (grated)
- 6 Cups Water

DIRECTIONS

1. Clean your escarole. Dirt tends to accumulate by the root so pay extra attention to clean thoroughly.
2. Squeeze out excess water and lay out flat on a paper towel.
3. Cut off the bottom of the stems and discard.
4. Cut the escarole leaves into bite sized pieces and set aside.
5. Remove casing from the sausage and break apart the meat.
6. Add 2 tbs of olive oil and meat to a large pot and sauté on medium heat until browned.
7. Reduce heat to low and add crushed garlic and a pinch of red pepper flakes.
8. Once garlic is golden, add the escarole, water, broth and beans.
9. Simmer on low for 20-30 minutes.
10. In a separate small sauce pot, fill with water and 2-3 tbs of salt and bring to a boil.
11. Add the pasta and cook al dente according to the package.
12. Transfer pasta with slotted spoon to the escarole pot.
13. Reserve the pasta water for the end if you want to thin out the soup.
14. Top each bowl with grated cheese and serve with warm bread.

Mangia é Statti Zitto!

ITALIAN WEDDING SOUP

 SERVES 8

Believe it or not this soup has nothing to do with weddings but more about the marriage of flavors. The combination of the different meats makes these little meatballs so delicious leaving them soft and tender while soaking in the broth. Growing up, we could always count on my mom to add this soup into the rotation. This is a fun soup to get the kids involved in.

INGREDIENTS

2 Pound Ground Beef
1 Pound Ground Pork
2 Cups Pecorino Ramano (grated)
¾ Cup Dried Parsley
¼ Cup Dried Basil
3 Garlic Cloves
1 Onion
Salt
Pepper
1 Pound Orzo Pasta
3 Cups Baby Spinach
1 Cup Flour
1 Qt Beef Broth
8 Cups Water
Extra Virgin Olive Oil

DIRECTIONS

1. In a large bowl, add meats, crushed garlic, basil, parsley, 1 ½ cups grated cheese and a pinch of salt and pepper.
2. Mix well to incorporate all ingredients.
3. Roll into bite sized balls.
4. In a separate bowl, add flour.
5. Roll the balls into the flour making sure to coat all sides.
6. Pour 2-3 tbs of olive oil into a frying pan on medium heat until oil is hot.
7. Fry the balls until brown on all sides.
8. Remove with slotted spoon and set aside.
9. In a large pot, add another 2-3 tbs of olive oil with chopped onions.
10. Sauté until translucent.
11. Keep on low simmer and add broth, 8 cups of water and spinach.
12. Slowly add the meatballs to the pot.
13. Keep on a low simmer for 30 minutes stirring occasionally.
14. Fill a small sauce pot with water and add 2 tbs of salt.
15. Bring to a boil.
16. Add orzo pasta and reduce to low heat.
17. Cook al dente according to the pasta package.
18. Remove pasta with slotted spoon and add to soup pot after soup is cooked.
19. Top each bowl with a sprinkle of grated cheese.

Mangia é Statti Zitto!

LENTIL SOUP

 SERVES 10-12

Lentil soup is typically considered a good luck soup. A tradition for New Years believed to bring good luck and wealth. The lentils symbolize a coin. This is also a perfect meatless soup for Fridays during Lent.

INGREDIENTS

1 Pound Lentils
1 Onion
2 Carrots
2 Stalks of Celery
2 Zucchini
Salt
Pepper
Red Pepper Flakes
2 Garlic Cloves
1 Tsp Dried Oregano
8 Cups Water
1 Qt Chicken Broth
Extra Virgin Olive Oil
Pecorino Ramano (grated)
½ Cup Fresh Chopped Parsley

DIRECTIONS

1. Wash and peel the carrots and zucchini.
2. Cut into bite sized pieces along with the celery and onion.
3. In a large pot, add 2 tbs of olive oil, all the vegetables and chopped garlic.
4. Sauté on medium-low heat until the vegetables start to brown.
5. Reduce heat to low and add in a pinch of red pepper flakes, oregano, salt and pepper.
6. Pour lentils into a strainer and rinse.
7. Remove pot from heat and transfer half of the vegetables to a blender.
8. Blend for 20 seconds until smooth.
9. Add the blended ingredients back to the pot.
10. Add water, broth and lentils.
11. Cook on low for 30 minutes stirring occasionally with a wooden spoon.
12. Serve with a drizzle of olive oil, parsley, grated cheese for a garnish.

Mangia é Statti Zitto!

PASTA FAGIOLI

 SERVES 8-10

If you're an Italian American from NY, this is pronounced pasta-fazool and is a perfect meal for those damp NY days. My grandparents could eat this soup any time of the year, even on the hottest days in summer. This soup was a staple in our household growing up. Now my kids love it. Can't go wrong with a classic!

INGREDIENTS

Extra Virgin Olive Oil
Red Pepper Flakes (optional)
1-2 Shallots
3 Garlic Cloves
2 Cans of Crushed Tomatoes
28 oz Chicken Broth
2-3 Tbs Fresh Chopped Parsley
1 Pound Ditalini Pasta
2 Cans of Cannellini Beans
Pecorino Romano Cheese (grated)
Black Pepper
¼ Cup Salt

Pro Tip: On occasion, we like to remove 4-6 sausage links from casing and add to the sauce pot as a first step.

DIRECTIONS

1. Coat your pot with extra virgin olive oil and put on low heat.
2. Add a few pinches of red pepper flakes for a little heat.
3. Add chopped shallots to the pot.
4. Sauté until shallots are translucent and add chopped garlic.
5. Sauté until brown then pour in crushed tomatoes.
6. Add chicken broth and let simmer on low heat for 30 minutes while stirring occasionally.
7. While the sauce is simmering, boil salted water in a separate pot for your ditalini pasta.
8. Cook until al dente, ~7-8 minutes.
9. Add parsley to the sauce pot.
10. Then using a slotted spoon, add the pasta to the sauce.
11. Save your pasta water to use if you need to thin out your sauce.
12. Drain and rinse the beans to add to the pasta.
13. Stir with a wooden spoon and let simmer for an additional 10 minutes.
14. Top each bowl with a little drizzle of extra virgin olive oil and serve with grated cheese, fresh parsley and black pepper.

Mangia é Statti Zitto!

ROASTED BUTTERNUT SQUASH SOUP

 SERVES 10-12

A fall favorite in our household. The smell of the roasted butternut squash will fill your home with a comforting aroma.

INGREDIENTS

- 3 Butternut Squash
- 5 Garlic Cloves
- 3 Carrots
- 2 Shallots
- 2 Tsp Sugar
- Salt
- Pepper
- 2-3 Cups Heavy or Light Cream
- 2 Tbs Butter
- 2 Cups Chicken or Vegetable Broth
- Extra Virgin Olive Oil
- Nutmeg

DIRECTIONS

1. Preheat oven to 375°F.
2. Cut your squash in half, removing the seeds and quartering it.
3. Season each piece with salt and pepper.
4. Roast in the oven at 375°F for 45 minutes or until the fork goes in with ease.
5. While the squash is in the oven, peel and cut up carrots and shallots.
6. Drizzle extra virgin olive oil in a pot on medium heat with a tbs of butter.
7. Add carrots and shallots, sugar and season with a pinch of both salt and pepper.
8. Place garlic on foil with a pinch of salt and roast in the oven for 20 mins.
9. Take out the squash and set aside to cool before removing the skin.
10. Remove the carrots and shallots from the pot and place in a blender or food processor with the roasted garlic and squash.
11. Add a tbs of butter to the pot and pour in the squash purée.
12. Slowly add the broth to the pot.
13. Stir and add cream.
14. Simmer on low for 20-25 minutes, stirring occasionally.
15. Serve hot with a pinch of nutmeg on top.

Mangia é Statti Zitto!

APPETIZERS

BURRATA WITH ROASTED TOMATOES & GARLIC

 SERVES 4-6

INGREDIENTS

1 Pound Red Grape Tomatoes
3 Garlic Cloves
1 Pound Burrata
¼ Cup Extra Virgin Olive Oil
Kosher Salt
Parchment Paper
Italian and/or Provolone Bread

DIRECTIONS

1. Preheat oven to 375°F.
2. Place tomatoes and garlic on baking sheet lined with parchment paper.
3. Sprinkle with a pinch of Kosher salt and drizzle olive oil.
4. Place in oven at 375°F for 20-25 minutes.
5. Remove baking sheet and gently mash tomatoes and garlic with a fork.
6. Place burrata on platter and cut in half.
7. Pour tomato, garlic and liquid on top of burrata.
8. Serve with warm sliced Italian or bread.

Mangia é Statti Zitto!

CALAMARI OREGANATA

 SERVES 8-10

Another delicious and easy "one pan" appetizer. I love this recipe because there is no mess since we aren't deep frying anything like other versions. Makes this dish healthier too!

INGREDIENTS

- 1 ½ Pounds Calamari Tubes
- ¼ Cup Seasoned Breadcrumbs
- ¼ Cup Pecorino Romano Cheese (grated)
- Extra Virgin Olive Oil
- 2-3 Garlic Cloves
- 2-3 Tbs Fresh Chopped Parsley
- 1 Lemon

DIRECTIONS

1. Preheat oven to 365°F.
2. Wash the calamari tubes and remove the cartilage, which feels like hard plastic.
3. Dry tubes well with paper towels and cut into rings.
4. Drizzle oil on pan to coat the bottom.
5. Place calamari rings on the pan.
6. Sprinkle on your cheese, breadcrumbs, crushed garlic and parsley.
7. Lightly mix to coat all the calamari.
8. Add another drizzle of extra virgin olive oil on top.
9. Place in oven at 365°F for no more than 7-8 minutes.
10. Serve with lemon wedges.

Mangia é Statti Zitto!

Easter Pie also known as Pizza Rustica or Pizza Di Pasqua is a delicious savory pie filled with meat and cheese. In my family we have always made this Easter week to enjoy on Easter Sunday. It has been a treasured tradition for many years. This can be made year round however there is something special about the feeling of anticipation. It makes this pie extra special. My paternal Grandparents always made this recipe in a large lasagna pan to feed a crowd. My maternal side along with my in laws have always made this in a pie plate and have made dozens at a time to give to the family. Both are equally delicious. I have always enjoyed making this with my mom and mother in law. This particular recipe is a combination from three Nonna's and aunts. Easter Pie is traditionally served at breakfast or as an appetizer. I hope you enjoy!

EASTER PIE

MAKES 2 PIES

INGREDIENTS

4 cups Flour
17 Eggs
2 Tlb Crisco or Butter
Pinch of salt
Ice Cold Water
2 lb. Ricotta
1/2 lb. Mozzarella
1 medium sized Soppresardo
1 large Dry Sweet Sausage
1/2 lb. Prosciutto
1/2 Cup Grated Pecorino Romano
Baking spray

Pro Tip: I like to make designs on the top of pie using leftover scraps of dough.

DIRECTIONS

1. Preheat oven to 350°F
2. Pour 2 cups of flour on the kitchen counter or work surface.
3. Add a pinch of salt
4. Make a well in the center
5. Whisk 2 eggs and carefully pour into the center.
6. Using fingers incorporate egg into flour.
7. Add 1 tablespoon of crisco or butter and work into flour.
8. Slowly add cold water 1 tablespoon at a time until you can form your dough into a ball.
9. Let ball of dough rest under cheesecloth while making second ball of dough.
10. Each ball will make a top and bottom to the pie.
11. For the filling
12. Fill a large bowl with warm water.
13. Soak soppresardo and dry sausage for a few minutes. This process will help with removing the skin.
14. Peel skin from meat and begin to cut all meat and mozzarella into bite sized pieces.
15. Whisk 12 eggs in a large bowl.
16. Add ricotta, grated cheese, mozzarella and all meats into the bowl.
17. Mix well.
18. Work with one dough at a time.
19. Dust countertop or work surface with a little four.
20. Cut dough in half and roll each piece out.
21. Spray pie plates and place dough down pressing dough into the pie plate.
22. Using a ladle fill pie plates with equal amounts of ricotta filling.
23. Place second layer of dough on top of filling.
24. Pinch the sides using thumb and forefinger.
25. Whisk 1 egg in small bowl and brush on the tops of pie for a golden crust.
26. Poke a few holes on the top of pie using a fork.
27. Bake in preheated 350°F oven for about 1 hour or until golden.
28. Let cool at least 30 minutes before cutting and serving

Mangia é Statti Zitto!

EGGPLANT ROLLATINI

 SERVES 8-10

Eggplant Rollatini is made up of thinly sliced eggplant that is fried to a light crisp before filling with creamy ricotta and ham. The eggplant is rolled and baked in marinara sauce. This is my mom's favorite and signature dish. I always requested this dish for my birthday growing up.

INGREDIENTS

- 2 Large Eggplants
- 4 Eggs
- 3 Cups Seasoned Breadcrumbs
- 2 Cups Pecorino Romano Cheese (grated)
- Salt
- Pepper
- ½ Cup Fresh Chopped Parsley
- 32 Oz Whole Milk Ricotta
- 2 Cups Mozzarella (shredded)
- 1 lb Sliced Ham
- 5 Cups Marinara Sauce
- Extra Virgin Olive Oil
- 2 Tbs Dried Basil

DIRECTIONS

1. Preheat oven to 350°F.
2. Skin the eggplant and cut into long thin slices.
3. Place eggs, ¼ cup of parsley, a pinch of both salt and pepper in one bowl and mix well.
4. In another bowl, add breadcrumbs and 1 cup of grated cheese and mix well.
5. Dip each slice of eggplant into the egg mixture and the breadcrumb mixture in that order.
6. Add olive oil to a frying pan on low heat.
7. Fry eggplant on both sides for a minute each.
8. Place fried eggplant slices on a paper towel to soak up any excess oil.
9. Mix Ricotta, 1 cup of grated cheese, ¼ cup of parsley, basil and shredded mozzarella in a large bowl.
10. Place 2 tbs of this mixture into the center of each eggplant slice. Add a slice of ham.
11. Put 2 cups of marinara sauce into a baking dish.
12. Roll the eggplant slices and place seam side down on the baking dish.
13. Pour the remaining marinara sauce over each eggplant roll.
14. Bake at 350°F for 25 minutes.

Mangia é Statti Zitto!

Eat N Shut Up | Appetizer | 45

FRIED BURRATA BOMBS

 SERVES 4

INGREDIENTS

½ Pound Prosciutto Di Parma
2 Burrata Balls
3 Eggs
1 Cup Flour
1 Cup Seasoned Breadcrumbs
¼ Cup Fresh Chopped Parsley
1 Cup Vegetable Oil
1 Cup Extra Virgin Olive Oil
Balsamic Glaze

DIRECTIONS

1. Set up 3 bowls. In one bowl, whisk eggs and add in parsley. The 2nd bowl is for flour and 3rd for breadcrumbs.
2. Start by laying out prosciutto, 3 vertical and 3 horizontal strips.
3. Place burrata in the center and wrap prosciutto around, covering the burrata.
4. Now, place burrata ball in the flour first, then into egg mixture and lastly into the breadcrumbs.
5. Pour oil into saucepan and bring to a sizzle.
6. Slowly add burrata one at a time, using a metal slotted spoon.
7. Fry until golden on all sides.
8. Take out and place on paper towel to absorb any excess oil.
9. When ready to serve, cut in half and add a drizzle of balsamic glaze.

Mangia é Statti Zitto!

MOZZARELLA IN CARROZZA

 SERVES 2

Mozzarella in Carrozza means mozzarella in a carriage. Think of this as an Italian Grilled Cheese Sandwich. This is typically served with either a basic marinara sauce or an anchovy and caper sauce.

INGREDIENTS

- 4 Slices White Bread (Preferably Arnold or Pepperidge Farm)
- 2 Eggs
- 2 Tbs Fresh Chopped Parsley
- ¾ Cup All Purpose Flour
- ½ Cup Plain or Seasoned Breadcrumbs
- 4 Slices Mozzarella
- 2 Tbs Extra Virgin Olive Oil
- 2 Tbs Butter
- ¼ Cup Pecorino Romano (grated)

Pro Tip: *For Anchovy Sauce, add 2 tablespoons of butter with a drizzle of extra virgin olive oil in a separate pan. Once butter starts to melt add 2 anchovy filets and a tablespoon of capers. Sauté for a few minutes on low heat until anchovies dissolve. Spoon over sandwich.*

DIRECTIONS

1. Remove crust from the bread and lay out on counter.
2. Use 2 slices of bread and 2 slices of mozzarella for each sandwich.
3. Gently press Mozzarella onto the bread.
4. Set up 3 bowls. In one bowl, beat eggs and add chopped parsley.
5. In the second bowl, add the flour.
6. In the third bowl, add grated cheese to your breadcrumbs.
7. Add butter and olive oil to a pan on low heat until butter is melted.
8. While pan is heating up, dip your sandwiches in the flour first, then the egg mixture and finally the breadcrumbs.
9. Place in your preheated pan and fry on both sides until a golden color.
10. Serve with sauce of choice.

Mangia é Statti Zitto!

PAN SEARED SCALLOPS

 SERVES 8-10

INGREDIENTS

1 Pound (~20) Sea Scallops
Extra Virgin Olive Oil
4 Tbs Butter
2 Garlic Cloves
1 Lemon
1 Sleeve Ritz Crackers
½ Cup Pecorino Romano Cheese (grated)
1 Tbs Fresh Chopped Parsley

Pro Tip: A great presentation for this dish is to serve on seashells

DIRECTIONS

1. Rinse scallops well.
2. Remove and discard the muscle. This is the small flap that's attached to the side of the muscle.
3. Place scallops on a paper towel and gently pat dry before setting aside.
4. Now start the crumb topping.
5. Crush Ritz crackers into crumbs.
6. In a skillet, melt 3 tbs butter and 1 tbs of olive oil.
7. Add 1 clove of crushed garlic and sauté on low until golden.
8. Add crumbs into the skillet and sauté on low until slightly toasted.
9. Add cheese and parsley and mix everything together.
10. Remove from heat and set aside before the next step.
11. Now heat a frying pan on medium heat and add 1 tbs of butter and 1 tbs of olive oil.
12. Add 1 clove of garlic and lemon wedges into center of pan and arrange the scallops around the pan.
13. Sear for one minute on medium and then flip the scallops to sear the other side for an additional minute.
14. Tilt the pan and spoon the butter, lemon and garlic juice on top of each scallop.
15. Transfer each scallop to a platter and top each one with 1 tsp of crumb mixture.

Mangia é Statti Zitto!

SCALLOPS SALTIMBOCCA

 SERVES 5

Saltimbocca means jumps in the mouth. These scallops are so delicious and flavorful, you are going to love them!

INGREDIENTS

- ½ Pound (~10-12) Sea Scallops
- 10-12 Sage Leaves
- ¼ Pound Prosciutto Di Parma
- 2 Tbs Butter
- 10-12 Toothpicks (optional)

DIRECTIONS

1. Wash scallops under cool water and remove the mussel. This is the little flap on the side of the scallop.
2. Lay out on a paper towel and gently pat down to dry.
3. Lay each piece of Prosciutto di Parma out, place 1 sage leaf in the center and add one scallop to each.
4. Gently tie a knot around scallop using each end of Prosciutto or you can wrap Prosciutto around scallop and secure it with a toothpick.
5. Add butter to a frying pan on medium to low heat. Once butter is melted, add 1 sage leaf to the center of the pan.
6. Add your scallop rolls to the pan in a circle towards the edge.
7. Cook for one minute, then flip over scallops for an additional minute.
8. Tilt pan and use a spoon to scoop up melted butter and place on each scallop.
9. Serve over creamy mashed potatoes or polenta.

Mangia é Statti Zitto!

SICILIAN STYLE STUFFED PEPPERS

 SERVES 4

INGREDIENTS

2 Red Bell Peppers
2 Garlic Cloves
½ Cup Black Cured Olives (pitted)
½ Pecorino Romano Cheese (grated)
2 Cups Seasoned Breadcrumbs
Extra Virgin Olive Oil
3 Anchovy Fillets
¾ Cup Chicken Broth
½ Cup Fresh Chopped Parsley
Red Pepper Flakes
Black Pepper

DIRECTIONS

1. Preheat oven to 350°F.
2. Clean the peppers and cut in half.
3. Remove seeds and ribs from the peppers.
4. Place the peppers on a baking sheet.
5. Coat a frying pan with olive oil on low heat.
6. Add crushed garlic, anchovies and a pinch of red pepper flakes to the pan.
7. Sauté until garlic turns golden and anchovies dissolve.
8. Cut pitted olives in half and add to the pan with breadcrumbs.
9. Sauté until breadcrumbs start to brown and remove from heat.
10. Add cheese, broth and parsley before mixing well.
11. Fill each pepper with the mixture.
12. Drizzle with olive oil.
13. Bake at 350°F for 25 minutes.

Mangia é Statti Zitto!

SPINACH ARTICHOKE DIP

 SERVES 10-12

INGREDIENTS

½ Pound Bacon
1 Large Onion
3 Packages of Frozen Creamed Spinach
2 Jars Artichoke Hearts
8 oz Cream Cheese
8 oz Pepperjack Cheese
½ Cup Heavy Cream
Non-Stick Cooking Spray

DIRECTIONS

1. Preheat oven to 350°F.
2. Cut the bacon into bite sized pieces and sauté until crispy and golden.
3. While bacon is sautéing, cut the onion into bize sized pieces.
4. Once bacon is done, remove from pan with slotted spoon and set aside.
5. Add the chopped onion into the same pan and sauté in the bacon fat until translucent.
6. Add thawed spinach, artichoke hearts, grated pepperjack cheese and cream cheese to the pan on low simmer until the cheese has melted.
7. Lastly add the heavy cream and mix well to incorporate all the ingredients.
8. Spray a baking dish with non-stick spray and pour the mixture into the dish.
9. Top with the bacon bits and bake at 350°F for 20 minutes.

Mangia é Statti Zitto!

STUFFED & FRIED SICILIAN OLIVES

 MAKES 36

Have you ever tried a stuffed, fried olive? This is an old Sicilian recipe from my Grandma/Nonna Matteo and my Aunt Nina. They were from Agrigento, Sicily. There are many variations with different meats and cheeses. This is how it was done in past generations.

INGREDIENTS

¼ Pound Ground Beef
¼ Pound Ground Pork
¼ Pound Prosciutto Di Parma
¼ Pound Ground Chicken
¾ Cup Chopped Carrots
¾ Cup Chopped Celery
¼ Cup Chopped Shallots
1 Lemon
4 Eggs
1 Cup All Purpose Flour
½ Cup White Wine
1 Cup Panko Breadcrumbs
3 Dozen Large Sicilian Green Olives
½ Cup Pecorino Romano Cheese (grated)
Extra Virgin Olive Oil

DIRECTIONS

1. Cut the Prosciutto into bite sized pieces and adding to a frying pan on medium heat.
2. Add chopped vegetables and sauté together in pan until browned.
3. Add wine and simmer on low until liquid evaporates.
4. Place contents into a food processor.
5. Next, add meat to the same pan and brown all meats together with the grated cheese.
6. Once browned, remove from pan and place in food processor with vegetables.
7. Add 2 egg yolks to the processor with lemon zest.
8. Blend all ingredients together until you get a paste like consistency.
9. Carefully remove the pit by butterflying the olives.
10. Take about a teaspoonful of the mixture and form a ball with your hand.
11. Mold the mixture into the pitted olive.
12. Have your frying pan heating up with olive oil.
13. Place flour, breadcrumbs and 2 beaten eggs into three separate bowls.
14. Start adding stuffed olives into the flour, then eggs and then breadcrumbs.
15. Slowly put the olives to the frying pan on low heat until golden.
16. Place on paper towels after frying to absorb any excess oil.
17. Plate and enjoy!

Mangia é Statti Zitto!

STUFFED CHERRY PEPPERS

 SERVES 4-6

An easy appetizer that my Dad loves and serves often.

INGREDIENTS

- 1 Large Jar of Cherry Peppers in Vinegar
- 2 Cups Seasoned Breadcrumbs
- 1 Cup Pecorino Romano Cheese (grated)
- 3 Anchovy Fillets
- 3 Garlic Cloves
- 2 Tbs Fresh Chopped Parsley
- 2-3 Tbs Extra Virgin Olive Oil
- 3 Tbs Butter

DIRECTIONS

1. Preheat oven to 350°F.
2. Cut off the tops of 15 peppers and remove the seeds.
3. Place peppers on a baking dish.
4. Mince the anchovies and crush the garlic.
5. In a large bowl, add all ingredients and mix well.
6. Stuff the peppers with the mixture.
7. Bake at 350°F for 15 minutes.
8. Place under broiler to crisp up the tops of the peppers for 2-3 minutes.

Mangia é Statti Zitto!

STUFFED MEATBALLS

 MAKES 24

INGREDIENTS

1 Pound Ground Pork

2 Pounds Ground Beef

½ Cup Dried Parsley

2 Tbs Fresh Chopped Parsley

2 Tbs Dried Basil

1 Cup Pecorino Romano Cheese (grated)

2 Eggs

1 Tsp Salt

½ Tsp Black Pepper

4 Garlic Cloves

2 Cups Seasoned Breadcrumbs

1 Pound Mozzarella

½ Pound Prosciutto Cotto or Ham

½ Loaf Italian Bread

2 Cups Milk

2+ Cups of Extra Virgin Olive Oil

DIRECTIONS

1. Preheat oven to 350°F.
2. Place garlic cloves on foil and drizzle with extra virgin olive oil and a pinch of salt.
3. Wrap foil around garlic, making a tent.
4. Place in oven at 350°F for 30-40 minutes or until golden.
5. While garlic is in the oven, place bread in a large bowl and pour milk over the bread to soak.
6. Take garlic out, mash with fork and add to softened bread.
7. Add meat, all the spices, eggs and cheese.
8. Mix well and make rounded balls with hands.
9. Slice mozzarella and Prosciutto into small square pieces that will fit inside the meatball.
10. Take each individual meatball, place in palm of hand and make a well with thumb.
11. Place one piece of ham and cheese inside the meatball and mold each meatball back into shape.
12. Then roll each meatball into seasoned breadcrumbs.
13. Fry in extra virgin olive oil on all sides. You may need to add extra olive oil during this cooking process.

Mangia é Statti Zitto!

STUFFED MUSHROOMS

 SERVES 8-10

Easy and perfect appetizer for any occasion. These have always been a staple in our family for every birthday, holiday or game day. They are quick, delicious and enough to feed a crowd.

INGREDIENTS

2 Dozen Mushrooms
1 Cup Pancetta
1 Shallot
3-4 Garlic Cloves
2 Cups Seasoned Breadcrumbs
2-3 Tbs Fresh Chopped Parsley
1 Cup Pecorino Romano Cheese (grated)
2-3 Cups Chicken Broth
Extra Virgin Olive Oil
1 Tbs of Butter

DIRECTIONS

1. Preheat oven to 350°F.
2. Wipe your mushrooms clean with cheesecloth or paper towels.
3. Then cut off the bottom of the stems and remove them from the caps.
4. Chop up the stems or place in a food processor.
5. Place mushroom caps on a baking dish.
6. Fry up the diced pancetta and add chopped shallot and chopped garlic.
7. Sauté until pancetta is crispy.
8. In a large bowl, add the seasoned breadcrumbs, the pancetta mixture, chopped mushroom stems, fresh parsley and Pecorino Romano. Mix well.
9. Gently pour in chicken broth a little at a time while mixing. You want a wet sand consistency.
10. Pour in a drizzle of extra virgin olive oil.
11. Mix and stuff the mushroom caps.
12. Brush each mushroom with a mixture of melted butter to 3 tbs extra virgin olive oil.
13. Bake 350°F for 20 minutes.

Mangia é Statti Zitto!

STUFFED PEPPERS & RICE SERVES 10-12

While this recipe is generally a great winter time comfort food, I always have an abundance of fryer peppers from the garden during summertime which makes this a multi seasonal delight.

INGREDIENTS

- 3 Cups White Rice
- 3 Cups Water
- 10-12 Green Fryer Peppers
- ½ Cup Fresh Chopped Parsley
- Ground Pepper
- Kosher Salt
- 1 ½ Cups Pecorino Romano Cheese (grated)
- Extra Virgin Olive Oil
- 2 Pounds Sweet Sausage
- 1 Large Onion
- 5-6 Garlic Cloves
- Red Pepper Flakes
- 1 Can of Crushed Tomatoes
- ½ Cup Red Wine
- 1 Cup Seasoned Breadcrumbs
- 4-5 Fresh Basil Leaves

DIRECTIONS

1. Preheat oven to 350°F.
2. Make 6 cups of white rice.
3. Put the rice in a large bowl and add parsley, pinch of ground pepper, pinch of Kosher salt, grated cheese and set aside.
4. Clean and cut off the tops of the peppers.
5. Cut a small sliver off the bottom of the peppers to let the steam out while cooking.
6. Remove inside ribs and tap upside down to remove the seeds.
7. Coat a pan with olive oil, place peppers in the pan and drizzle olive oil on top of the peppers.
8. Sprinkle kosher salt on the peppers and bake them for 25 minutes at 350°F.
9. While the peppers are in the oven, add the sausage meat, chopped onion, chopped garlic and red pepper flakes to a skillet and sauté until the sausage is fully cooked and browned.
10. Add crushed tomatoes, basil leaves and red wine (once around the pot) and simmer on low heat for 20 minutes.
11. Take the peppers out of the oven and let them cool.
12. Pour sauce mixture over rice and add seasoned breadcrumbs.
13. Mix well and start stuffing peppers.
14. Place stuffed peppers on baking sheet and bake for 30-40 minutes at 350°F.

Mangia é Statti Zitto!

SIDES

ARANCINI

 SERVES 8-10

Refer to the Risotto recipe for the rice (page 77). Arancini are usually longer or bigger and stuffed with meat and peas. This is a traditional Sicilian Street food.

INGREDIENTS

¼ Cup Extra Virgin Olive Oil

4 Eggs

2 Cups Flour

Pinch Of Salt

Pinch Of Pepper

3 Cups Breadcrumbs

2+ Cups Vegetable Oil

¼ Cup Pecorino Romano Cheese (grated)

2-3 Tbs Fresh Chopped Parsley

2 Pounds Ground Beef

2 Cups Crushed Tomatoes

1 Cup Frozen Peas

Pro Tip: Depending on the percentage of fat in the ground beef you might have to drain out some grease after browning on step 4.

DIRECTIONS

1. Refer to the Risotto recipe to make the rice.
2. Add 3 tbs of olive oil in the frying pan.
3. Add ground beef.
4. Once beef is browned, add crushed tomatoes, salt, pepper and simmer for 15 minutes.
5. Mix in the frozen peas and set aside to cool.
6. Form rice into balls and make an indent with your thumb.
7. Place a tbs of meat into the center of the rice ball.
8. Set up 3 bowls. One for flour, one for whisked eggs and last for breadcrumbs.
9. Coat each ball in that order.
10. In a frying pan, add 2 cups of vegetable oil. Turn the burner to a medium heat.
11. Once heated, add the rice balls slowly with a slotted spoon one at a time.
12. Turn the rice balls to crisp all sides. Add more vegetable oil to the pan as needed when frying up the rice balls.
13. Remove the rice balls from the pan and sprinkle with shredded parsley and more grated cheese.

Mangia é Statti Zitto!

ASPARAGUS WITH BÉCHAMEL SAUCE

 SERVES 8-10

This is such a delicious and elegant side to any fish or meat dish.

INGREDIENTS

3 Bunches Of Asparagus
Extra Virgin Olive Oil
Salt
Pepper
1 Cup Water
2 Tbs Butter
¼ Cup Flour
1 ½ Cups Heavy Or Light Cream
Nutmeg
1 Lemon
½ Pound Prosciutto Di Parma

DIRECTIONS

1. Preheat oven to 350ºF.
2. Clean your asparagus and cut about an inch off the ends.
3. Place in a baking dish and drizzle extra virgin olive oil on top.
4. Season with salt and pepper.
5. Pour the water around the edges of the baking dish.
6. Cover with foil, poke a few holes and place in the oven for 15 -18 minutes at 350ºF.
7. While the asparagus is in the oven, start your sauce.
8. Place the butter in a saucepan on low heat.
9. Once melted, add in flour and whisk well until thick.
10. Pour in light or heavy cream and whisk until creamy smooth with no lumps.
11. Add in a pinch or 2 of nutmeg.
12. Take asparagus out of the oven and squeeze one lemon on top.
13. Slowly pour sauce on top of asparagus.
14. Cut up the prosciutto into thin ribbons and place on top.
15. Place the dish back in the oven for 5 minutes.
16. Plate and enjoy!

POLENTA

 SERVES 2-4

Polenta is a simple dish made of boiled cornmeal and only takes a few ingredients to make. It's so versatile, you can make this for breakfast with butter, lunch with marinara sauce or dinner with braciole or meat sauce. Polenta will always remind me of my Grandparents.

INGREDIENTS

1 Cup Yellow Cornmeal
4 Cups Water
½ Tsp Salt
Extra Virgin Olive Oil
2 Tbs Butter
Parmigiano Romano for Garnish
1 Cup Marinara Sauce

DIRECTIONS

1. Add the water to a pot and bring to a boil.
2. Slowly add in the cornmeal while whisking.
3. Remove from heat and whisk until there are no lumps.
4. Add salt.
5. Place on low to medium heat for 20-30 minutes.
6. While it's cooking, whisk anytime bubbles start to form.
7. Remove from heat when polenta becomes thick.
8. Use a wooden spoon to scrape the sides and bottom of the pot.
9. Add butter and serve immediately with either butter, sauce or meat.

Mangia é Statti Zitto!

RED, WHITE AND BLUE POTATOES

 SERVES 8-10

A fun side to any meat or fish dish, especially on patriotic holidays.

INGREDIENTS

1 ½ Pounds Red, White and Blue Potatoes
Extra Virgin Olive Oil
2 Large Lemons
3 Springs Fresh Rosemary
Salt
Pepper

DIRECTIONS

1. Preheat the oven to 375°F.
2. Pour a ½ cup of olive oil onto a sheet pan.
3. Slice the potatoes in half to help infuse the lemon juice.
4. Arrange the potatoes in a single layer on the sheet pan making sure not to overlap.
5. Season with salt, pepper and juice from 1 lemon.
6. Gently toss the potatoes to coat.
7. Add rosemary on top.
8. Slice the 2nd lemon and arrange evenly on the pan.
9. Bake at 375°F for 40 minutes.
10. Remove from the oven and flip the potatoes using a spatula.
11. Drizzle more olive oil over the potatoes and bake for an additional 15 minutes until fork tender.

Mangia é Statti Zitto!

RISOTTO

 SERVES 8

Risotto is a classic Italian rice dish. This rice is thick and creamy and is the perfect recipe to form the rice balls on both the Arancini and Suppli recipes.

INGREDIENTS

16 Oz Container of Chicken Broth
8 Cups Water
1 Large Onion
3 Cups Arborio Rice
2 Cups White Wine
¼ Cup Pecorino Romano Cheese (grated)

Pro Tip: Risotto can be served as a main meal. My family also enjoys it when I add asparagus or shrimp.

DIRECTIONS

1. Add water and chicken broth to a large pot and bring to a boil.
2. Reduce heat to simmer.
3. Next, add 3 tbs of olive oil to a deep skillet and start to fry the chopped onions.
4. Once the onions are browned, add the Arborio rice all at once.
5. Once the rice is toasted, add the white wine and stir until the liquid dissolves.
6. Begin adding the broth slowly, adding 1 ladle of broth at a time.
7. Once all liquid is absorbed into the rice, mix in ¾ of the grated cheese.
8. Set the rice aside to let it cool. The rice should be soft and plump.

Mangia é Statti Zitto!

SAUTEED CABBAGE WITH PANCETTA

 SERVES 4-6

This recipe will make everyone a fan of cabbage. It is so delicious!!! Everyone will be coming back for seconds. Great dish for lunch or a side to accompany any meat dish.

INGREDIENTS

1 Tbs Butter
½ Cup Pancetta
1 Shallot (chopped)
Red Pepper Flakes
3 Garlic Cloves
1 Large Head of Cabbage
2 Cups Chicken Broth
Pepper
1 Tbs Fresh Chopped Parsley

DIRECTIONS

1. Add butter to the pan and keep on low heat.
2. Once melted, add in your chopped pancetta.
3. Sauté until crispy then add in the chopped shallot.
4. Sauté for a few more minutes and add in a few pinches of red pepper flakes before adding the chopped garlic.
5. Keep on low heat for the next few steps.
6. Chop up one head of cabbage and add to the pan.
7. Pour in chicken broth and ground pepper.
8. Place the lid on the pan and just stir occasionally. Cabbage will start to wilt and soak up all those delicious flavors.
9. Once all broth is evaporated (about 35 minutes), you can serve.
10. Mix well and plate.
11. Chop some fresh parsley for garnish.

Mangia é Statti Zitto!

STUFFED ARTICHOKES

 SERVES 4

Stuff Artichokes takes me back to my childhood. I have beautiful memories of my mom and grandma making these for Easter and Thanksgiving. These have always been a family favorite. I can honestly say these are the best artichokes I have ever eaten.

INGREDIENTS

- 4 Artichokes
- 4 Cups Seasoned Breadcrumbs
- 8 Garlic Cloves
- 1 Qt Chicken Broth
- 4 Tbs Fresh Chopped Parsley
- 1 Cup Pecorino Romano (grated)
- ¾ Cups Extra Virgin Olive Oil

Pro Tip: In recent years on occasion we like to fry up bite sized pieces of bacon or pancetta and add to stuffing mix.

DIRECTIONS

1. Soak the artichokes in a large bowl or pot with cool water for at least 20 minutes.
2. Using scissors, trim the tops of the artichoke leaves.
3. Turn artichokes upside down and bang on cutting board to loosen up all the leaves.
4. Gently spread all the leaves apart by hand and set aside.
5. In a separate large bowl, add breadcrumbs, chopped garlic, parsley, grated cheese, 2 cups of chicken broth and ¼ cup of olive oil.
6. Mix all together. I like to use my hands to mix to feel the consistency. The mixture should have a wet sand consistency.
7. If needed, add chicken broth and olive oil a tbs at a time to get the right consistency.
8. Stuff every leave with the mixture starting with the outer leaves.
9. Place artichokes into a large pot and fill the pot with equal amounts of water to chicken broth until it reaches halfway up the artichokes. You might need two pots to fit all the artichokes.
10. Place the pots on low heat covered for at least 60 minutes.
11. As the liquid evaporates, you might need to add more to the pot.
12. The artichokes are done when the leaves pull off with ease. If not, cook longer. This can take up to two hours depending on how big they are.

Mangia é Statti Zitto!

STUFFED CABBAGE

 SERVES 10-12

Stuffed cabbage is made by many different cultures around the world. Each country has their own unique recipe with meats and spices. I hope you enjoy my Italian version. This is a hearty comfort meal packed with flavor.

INGREDIENTS

- 1 Head of Cabbage
- 3 Carrots
- 2 Shallots
- 3 Garlic Cloves
- 1 Pound Sausage
- 3-4 Slices of White Bread or a Half Loaf of Italian Bread
- 2 Cups Whole Milk
- 1 Cup Pecorino Romano Cheese (grated)
- 8 Cups Marinara Sauce
- ¼ Cup Salt

Pro Tip: Works great with day or two old Italian bread. Breadcrumbs can be used instead of bread soaked in milk.

DIRECTIONS

1. Preheat oven to 350°F.
2. Carefully cut the core out of the cabbage and placing in a large pot of salted water.
3. Boil until leaves are tender.
4. Remove the leaves and place in a bowl of cold water.
5. Once the leaves are cool, lay on paper towel and pat dry.
6. In the food processor, add the carrots, shallots and garlic.
7. Pulse the carrot mix until puréed.
8. Next, sauté your pancetta.
9. Once crispy, remove from pan and place in a large bowl.
10. To that same pan, add your sausage and carrot mix.
11. Cook until sausage is browned and add to the bowl.
12. I soak a few pieces of bread in milk until it becomes mushy and add it to the bowl.
13. Add grated cheese and mix well.
14. Fill the dry cabbage leaves with the stuffing mix and roll tight.
15. Place in a baking pan seam side down with sauce on bottom and a ladle of sauce on top of each roll.
16. Bake at 350°F for 30-40 minutes.

Mangia é Statti Zitto!

SUPPLI

SERVES 10-12

Refer to the Risotto recipe (page 77) for the rice balls. Suppli are smaller than Arancini and stuffed with mozzarella.

INGREDIENTS

1 Pound Fresh Mozzarella Cheese

4 Eggs

Pinch of Salt

Pinch of Pepper

3 Cups Breadcrumbs

2-3 Cups Flour

2 Cups Vegetable Oil

1/4 Cup Pecorino Romano Cheese (grated)

2-3 Tbs Fresh Chopped Parsley

DIRECTIONS

1. Refer to the Risotto recipe for the rice balls.
2. Cut up fresh mozzarella into small cubes.
3. Roll the rice into small balls and add one cube into the center of the ball.
4. Once all of the balls are formed, prepare 3 bowls with an egg mixture with salt and pepper in one, breadcrumbs in another and flour in the last bowl.
5. Coat the balls in the flour, egg mixture and breadcrumbs in that order and set aside.
6. Using a frying pan, add 2 cups of vegetable oil. Turn the burner to a medium heat.
7. Once heated, add the rice balls slowly with a slotted spoon one at a time.
8. Turn the rice balls to crisp all sides. Add more vegetable oil to the pan as needed when frying up the rice balls.
9. Remove the rice balls from the pan and sprinkle with shredded parsley and more grated cheese.

Mangia é Statti Zitto!

PASTA

AUNT CONCETTA'S MANICOTTI

 SERVES 10-12

Manicotti is made of a thin pasta crepe that is soft and filled with creamy ricotta. The crepes are covered in marinara sauce and baked. I always think of my Grandma/Nonna Matteo and Aunt Concetta when making this dish.

INGREDIENTS

1 ¼ Cups All Purpose Flour

1 ½ Cups Water

1 Egg

Extra Virgin Olive Oil

3 Pounds Whole Milk Ricotta

¼ Cup Fresh Chopped Parsley

2 Tbs Fresh Chopped Basil

½ Cup Pecorino Romano (grated)

1 Cup Mozzarella (grated)

6 Cups Premade Marinara Sauce

Fresh Black Pepper

DIRECTIONS

1. Preheat oven to 350°F.
2. Add the flour, water and egg to a large bowl.
3. Whisk. You should have a thin batter. If not, add a little more water.
4. Using a 6" nonstick frying pan, add a tsp of olive oil on medium heat.
5. Rotate the pan to coat all sides.
6. Add ⅓ cups of the batter to the pan and rotate to spread a thin layer.
7. When the edges start to curl up, flip for an additional 20 seconds.
8. Repeat these steps for 10-12 shells. These can be made up to a day in advance.
9. For the filling, mix the ricotta, parsley, basil, grated cheese, mozzarella and black pepper in a large bowl.
10. Spread 2 cups of marinara sauce evenly on a baking dish.
11. Add a ½ cup of the filling to each shell.
12. Roll the shells and place seam side down on a baking dish.
13. Pour just enough marinara sauce over each shell to cover them.
14. Bake at 350°F for 35-40 minutes.
15. Garnish with parsley and a little extra grated cheese.

BROCCOLI RABE WITH SAUSAGE & ORECCHIETTE

 SERVES 7-8

INGREDIENTS

3 Bunches Broccoli Rabe

2 Pounds Sweet Sausage

1 Pound Hot Sausage

1 Qt Chicken Broth

3 Garlic Cloves

1 Pound Orecchiette

Red Pepper Flakes

Extra Virgin Olive Oil

Salt

Pepper

Parmigiano Reggiano

Italian Bread

DIRECTIONS

1. Add 2-3 tbs of salt to a large pot of water and bring to a boil.
2. Wash broccoli rabe 2-3 times.
3. Cut 1-2 inches off the broccoli rabe stems and discard.
4. Blanch broccoli rabe quickly in the boiling water for 2-3 minutes. This process takes the bitterness out.
5. Remove with tongs and place on cloth to cool.
6. Now add the orecchiette pasta to the pot and cook al dente according to the package. You can use a separate pot of boiling water if you prefer.
7. In a deep skillet, add 2 tbs of olive oil on medium heat.
8. Remove the sausage from the casing and add to the skillet until browned.
9. Add a pinch of red pepper flakes and minced garlic.
10. Reduce skillet heat to low.
11. Cut broccoli rabe into 1-2 inch pieces and add to the skillet with the chicken broth.
12. Transfer the pasta with a slotted spoon into the skillet. Reserve some of the pasta water for later.
13. Keep the skillet on low heat for an additional 5 minutes to incorporate all of the flavors.
14. Add a ladle or two of the pasta water until you get the desired "saucy-ness".
15. Serve with warm Italian bread and garnish with Parmigiano Reggiano.

Mangia é Statti Zitto!

CALAMARATA PASTA WITH ITALIAN TUNA & TOMATO SAUCE

 SERVES 7-8

INGREDIENTS

1 Pound Calamarata Pasta

4-5 Garlic Cloves

1 Jar Italian Tuna

1 Jar Mutti Puree Tomato Sauce

4-5 Anchovy Fillets

¾ Cup Sicilian Green Olives (pitted)

Red Pepper Flakes

2 Tbs Fresh Chopped Parsley

2-3 Tbs Salt

2-3 Tbs Extra Virgin Olive Oil

DIRECTIONS

1. Add the salt to a large pot of water and bring to a boil.
2. In a large skillet on low heat, add olive oil, anchovies and sliced garlic.
3. Once the anchovies have dissolved and garlic is browned, add a pinch of red pepper flakes.
4. Add the sauce and sliced olives to the skillet on low heat and stir with wooden spoon.
5. Water should be boiling at this point. Cook the pasta al dente according to the package instructions.
6. Add tuna to the skillet and simmer on low for 10 minutes.
7. Using a slotted spoon, transfer the pasta to the skillet.
8. Garnish with parsley.

Mangia é Statti Zitto!

GNOCCHI

 SERVES 7-8

This is a homemade rustic dish and not every piece needs to look the same. This is probably the easiest pasta to make. Each bite is soft, and delicious.

INGREDIENTS

5-6 Yukon Gold Potatoes
2 Eggs
1 Cup 00 Flour
1 Stick Butter
Salt
2-3 Sage Leaves
2-3 Cups Marinara Sauce (optional)

DIRECTIONS

1. Add 4-5 tbs of salt to a large pot of water and bring it to a boil.
2. Once the water is boiling, add the whole potatoes with the skin on to the pot on medium heat.
3. Check if the potatoes are done by inserting a fork into the thickest part of the potato. If it goes in with ease, they are done.
4. Transfer potatoes with tongs into a large bowl.
5. Once potatoes are slightly cool, remove the skin with your hands.
6. Mash the potatoes well using a handheld masher or an electric whisk leaving no lumps.
7. Dust a few tbs of flour onto the counter.
8. Place the potatoes onto the flour and make a well in the center of the mound.
9. Whisk eggs and a teaspoon of salt in a separate bowl. Pour into the well.
10. Slowly add flour and hand mix until you're able to form a stable ball.
11. Cut into 4 equal pieces.
12. Bring another pot of salted water to a boil.
13. Roll each quarter into a 10-12 inch log.
14. Using a butter knife, cut the logs into ½ inch to 1 ½ inch pieces.
15. Gently roll each piece along the back side of a fork to imprint the lines.
16. Sprinkle flour onto the Gnocchi pieces and let sit for 2-5 minutes.
17. Melt the butter with sage leaves in a saucepan on low heat.
18. Add Gnocchi into the pot with light boiling water.
19. Transfer the batch of Gnocchi into a bowl and drizzle either the butter or marinara sauce over the top.
20. Repeat the last 2 steps until each batch of 4-5 Gnocchi is in their own bowl.

Mangia é Statti Zitto!

GNUDI

 SERVES 7-8

This is not a dish you typically see on a menu but my Grandma/Nonna Matteo made this on occasion. They are basically the delicious filling of ravioli or manicotti. Her version always incorporated spinach, but you may choose to leave it out.

INGREDIENTS

2 Pounds Ricotta

½ Cup Parmigiano Reggiano

½ Cup Frozen Spinach (optional)

2 Cups Flour

½ Cup Plain Breadcrumbs

4 Tbs Butter

3 Sage Leaves

4 Cups Marinara Sauce (optional)

Salt

Pepper

Pro Tip: Fresh baby spinach can be used in place of frozen. Boil the spinach and drain well.

DIRECTIONS

1. Add ricotta, thawed/drained spinach, grated Parmigiano Reggiano, ⅓ cups of flour and breadcrumbs to a large bowl and mix well.
2. Cover with plastic wrap and place in refrigerator for at least 30 minutes.
3. Add 2-3 tbs of salt to a large pot of water and bring to a boil.
4. Place the remaining flour in a baking dish.
5. In a saucepan, melt butter and sage leaves. Keep on low heat.
6. Remove the bowl out of the refrigerator and start rolling into balls roughly the size of a golf ball.
7. Roll the balls in the flour to coat all sides.
8. Using a slotted spoon, carefully lower 4-5 balls into the boiling water.
9. When they float to the top, remove and plate with a drizzle of the melted butter or a little marinara sauce.
10. Continue the last two steps until all the balls are served.

Mangia é Statti Zitto!

LASAGNA

 SERVES 8-10

Lasagna is a classic baked pasta dish with delicious layers of sauce and cheeses. Rest assured this meal was on our table for most holidays. Meat can be added between the layers as well.

INGREDIENTS

- 2 Packages Fresh Lasagna Sheets
- 3 Pounds Fresh Ricotta
- 2 Eggs
- 6 Cups Shredded Mozzarella
- ½ Cup Fresh Chopped Parsley
- 1 Cup Pecorino Romano Cheese (Grated)
- 5-6 Basil Leaves
- Black Pepper
- Salt
- 8-10 Cups Marinara Sauce
- Extra Virgin Olive Oil

DIRECTIONS

1. Preheat oven to 350°F.
2. Salt a large pasta pot and bring to a boil.
3. Add pasta sheets to the boiling water.
4. Cook according to package instructions.
5. Remove from pot and place in a bowl of cold water.
6. In a large bowl, add ricotta, eggs, parsley, chopped basil, 3 cups of mozzarella, Pecorino Romano cheese, a pinch of black pepper and mix well.
7. Add a ladle of the marinara sauce to a 9"x13" baking dish.
8. Drizzle olive oil.
9. Place a layer of pasta followed by a layer of sauce and a layer of ricotta mix.
10. Continue placing these layers until you get to the top of the pan.
11. Cover the whole lasagna with a layer of sauce and bake for 30 minutes.
12. Remove from oven and sprinkle the remainder of the mozzarella on top.
13. Bake for an additional 30 minutes.
14. Let cool before serving.

Mangia é Statti Zitto!

LINGUINE & CLAMS

 SERVES 8-10

INGREDIENTS

2-3 Dozen Little Neck Clams

1 Cup White Wine

1 Cup IPA Beer

2 Shallots

3-4 Garlic Cloves

2-3 Tbs Salt

1 Pound Linguine

2 Cans of Chopped Clams (optional)

1 Handful Fresh Chopped Parsley

Extra Virgin Olive Oil

Pinch of Red Pepper Flakes

1 Tbs Butter

Pro Tip: *I like to serve on a platter with a dozen clams circling the pasta.*

DIRECTIONS

1. Salt a large pot of water for the Linguine and bring it to a boil.
2. While that is heating up, rinse the clams well in a large bowl of cold water.
3. Add the clams, beer and ½ cup of wine to a deep skillet on medium heat.
4. As clams start to open, remove them with a slotted spoon and set aside.
5. In a medium size saucepan, add the olive oil on low heat.
6. Once pan is heated, sauté chopped shallots, salt, butter and red pepper flakes until shallots turn translucent.
7. The pot of water should be boiling by now, add the Linguine and cook al dente according to the package.
8. At this point, the clams should have cooled. Remove the clams from the shells and discard the shells. You can chop up the clams if you prefer.
9. Crush the garlic cloves and add them to the saucepan. Keep on low heat until golden.
10. Add the other ½ cup of wine, clams and parsley to the saucepan. If you would like extra clams, you can add cans of clams.
11. Simmer on low for 5 minutes.
12. Transfer the Linguine with tongs to a large bowl and pour clam sauce over the top.
13. Garnish with parsley.

Mangia é Statti Zitto!

LOBSTER & SHRIMP FRA DIAVOLO

 SERVES 6-8

Lobster Fra Diavolo is a seafood dish featuring lobster meat in a rich and spicy tomato sauce.

INGREDIENTS

4 Lobster Tails

½ Pound Large Shrimp

Large Onion

Salt

Pepper

½ Tsp Cayenne Pepper

1 Long Hot Pepper

3 Cloves Garlic

1 Can Whole Peeled Tomatoes

¼ Cup Flour

1 Cup White Wine

¼ Cup Fresh Chopped Parsley

2 Tbs Butter

¼ Cup Extra Virgin Olive Oil

Pinch of Red Pepper Flakes

1 Pound Fresh Fettuccine

Pro Tip: Fresh pasta cooks quicker. To make this dish gluten free, omit the flour (used for thickening sauce) and use a gluten free pasta

DIRECTIONS

1. Clean, de-vein and remove the tails from the shrimp. Discard the tails.
2. Cut the lobster tails to remove the meat making sure to keep the meat intact with the shell.
3. Pat the shrimp and lobster down with paper towels to remove all moisture.
4. Place both the lobster and shrimp in a large bowl before seasoning with salt, pepper, cayenne pepper and flour.
5. Mix well to ensure every piece is coated with the seasoning.
6. In a deep skillet, add butter and olive oil.
7. Simmer on low until butter is melted and add the shrimp and lobster.
8. Sauté for two to three minutes on both sides.
9. Remove from pan and set aside.
10. To the same skillet, sauté chopped onion, garlic, chopped long hot pepper and red pepper flakes.
11. Cut the lobster meat into bite sized pieces and discard the shells.
12. Gently crush tomatoes by hand and add with the wine to skillet.
13. Let simmer for 20 minutes.
14. Now add a 2-3 tbs of salt to a large pot of water before bringing to a boil for the pasta.
15. When there is about 5 minutes left on the simmer, add the shrimp and lobster meat to the skillet.
16. Now add the fettuccine to the boiling water and follow the package instructions to cook al dente.
17. Remove pasta from pot onto serving plates and pour sauce over top.
18. Sprinkle parsley for garnish.

Mangia é Statti Zitto!

PASTA ALLA NORMA

 SERVES 6-8

Pasta Alla Norma is a classic and delicious Sicilian dish. My grandparents had incredible gardens with a surplus of eggplant which we enjoyed many different ways.

INGREDIENTS

1 Large Eggplant
3 Anchovy Fillets
1 Onion
1 Pound Rigatoni
2 Garlic Cloves
1 Can of Crushed Tomatoes
Pinch of Red Pepper Flakes
¼ Cup Extra Virgin Olive Oil
2-3 Tbs Salt

DIRECTIONS

1. Salt a large pot of water for the rigatoni and bringing it to a boil.
2. While water is heating up, cut the eggplant into bite sized pieces. I like to leave some of the skin on.
3. Now, add the olive oil to a skillet and keep on medium to low heat.
4. Add the eggplant to the skillet until all sides are browned.
5. While eggplant is cooking, grate the onion and slice the garlic.
6. Your pot of water should be boiling by now. Add the rigatoni and cook al dente according to the package.
7. Remove eggplant with a slotted spoon and set aside on a paper towel.
8. To the same skillet, add the onion, anchovies and garlic on low heat.
9. Once anchovies liquify and the garlic starts to brown, add the tomatoes.
10. Cook on low heat until rigatoni is cooked.
11. Transfer rigatoni with a slotted spoon to the skillet and toss to evenly coat. Reserve the pasta water just in case you want to thin out the pasta at the end.
12. Add the eggplant to the skillet and gently toss together.

Mangia é Statti Zitto!

PENNE ALLA VODKA

 SERVES 6-8

Here is your typical Italian American dish. You can find this across most states. You will love making this easy flavorful dish for your family and friends. Sure to feed a crowd!

INGREDIENTS

- 2-3 Tbs Salt
- 1 Large Onion
- 1 Tbs Sugar
- 3 Garlic Cloves
- ½ Cup Sundried Tomatoes
- 1 Can Crushed Tomatoes
- 1½ Cups Heavy Cream
- 1 Cup Pecorino Romano (grated)
- ¼ Cup Vodka
- Red Pepper Flakes
- 2 Tbs Sugar
- Fresh Black Pepper
- 1 Tsp Kosher Salt
- 4-5 Slices Prosciutto Di Parma
- 1 Pound Penne Pasta
- Fresh Basil
- Extra Virgin Olive Oil

DIRECTIONS

1. Salt a large pot of water and bring to a boil.
2. In a deep skillet add 2 tbs extra virgin oil on medium heat.
3. Add chopped onion, 2 pinches of red pepper flakes and season with Kosher salt and pepper.
4. Mix with a wooden spoon and add sugar. The sugar will caramelize the onions.
5. Sauté for a few minutes until the onions start to brown.
6. Add sliced garlic and sauté until golden.
7. Take pan off heat and add vodka, stir with wooden spoon and place back on heat.
8. Add crushed tomatoes, sundried tomatoes, cream, and grated cheese. Mix well.
9. Your water should be boiling at this point. Turn the heat down to medium.
10. Add your pasta and cook al dente according to the package instructions.
11. Using a slotted spoon, transfer the pasta to the skillet. Mix well to coat all of the pasta.
12. Cut the Prosciutto into ribbons and place over the top of the pasta.
13. Garnish with basil and extra grated cheese.

Mangia é Statti Zitto!

PUTTANESCA

 SERVES 6-8

The Bold Story of Puttanesca
Don't let the name scare you—Puttanesca is as fun to eat as it is to say. Puttanesca comes from the Italian word puttana. Legend has it this fiery pasta was thrown together by resourceful women (the ladies of the night) in Naples using whatever bold, salty ingredients they had in their kitchens—quick, easy, and satisfying between, let's just say..."social appointments". Whether the story is fact or folklore, one thing's for sure: this dish is fast, fabulous, and a little bit scandalous—in the best way.

INGREDIENTS

- ¼ Cup Extra Virgin Olive Oil
- 1 Cup Mixed Olives (Black Cured, Kalamata and Sicilian Green)
- 3 Garlic Cloves
- 3 Tbs Capers
- 3-4 Anchovy Fillets (from a jar)
- 1 Can Whole Peeled Tomatoes
- 2-3 Tbs Fresh Chopped Parsley
- 2-3 Tbs Salt
- Pinch of Red Pepper Flakes
- 1 Pound Spaghetti

DIRECTIONS

1. Salt a large pot of water for the spaghetti and bringing it to a boil.
2. In the meantime, add olive oil and garlic to a skillet on low until garlic is browned, not burned.
3. Keep the skillet on low heat during these next steps.
4. Add the anchovies into the skillet. Measure out a tbs of the oil inside the anchovy jar and add to the skillet.
5. Add red pepper flakes.
6. Using a wooden spoon, mix the anchovies until they dissolve.
7. Break tomatoes apart by hand before adding them to the skillet.
8. Chop up the olives and add to the skillet with capers.
9. Lastly, add fresh parsley.
10. At this point, the water should be boiling. Add in your spaghetti and cook al dente.
11. Transfer spaghetti from the pot to the skillet while reserving the water.
12. Toss the skillet well to coat spaghetti.
13. Add one ladle at a time of the spaghetti water to the skillet until you get the "saucy-ness" you desire.
14. Garnish with parsley if you desire.

Mangia é Statti Zitto!

QUICK MARINARA SAUCE

MAKES 5-6 CUPS

A foundational sauce to have on hand for endless recipes. Get back to the basics and leave the jars on the store shelf.

INGREDIENTS

3 Cans Crushed Tomatoes

3 Garlic Cloves

Red Pepper Flakes

3 Tbs Extra Virgin Olive Oil

¼ Cup Fresh Chopped Parsley

4-5 Basil Leaves

1 Onion

2 Tbs Sugar

Salt

Pepper

Splash of Red Wine (optional)

DIRECTIONS

1. Pour olive oil in a large saucepot on low heat.
2. Chop up an onion and add to the pot sauté until translucent.
3. Season with salt, pepper and sugar and keep on low heat for 5-8 minutes.
4. Add garlic cloves, sauté until golden.
5. Add a pinch of red pepper flakes.
6. Pour in the tomatoes, red wine, basil and parsley, simmer for 20-30 minutes on low heat.

Mangia é Statti Zitto!

SPAGHETTI AGLIO E'ALICI

 SERVES 8

It has always been tradition to make this simple and delicious meal on the feast of San Giuseppe. Saint Joseph was the earthly father to Jesus and a carpenter which is why we toast the breadcrumbs to represent the saw dust. This is a delicious and rustic dish, traditional for St. Joseph's Day. A favorite for both of my grandfathers, Modestino and Giuseppe.

INGREDIENTS

- 3-4 Garlic Cloves
- ¼ Cup Extra Virgin Olive Oil
- 4-5 Anchovy Fillets in a Jar
- 1 Tbs Butter
- ¼ Cup White Wine (optional)
- 4 Tbs Fresh Chopped Parsley
- 1 Pound Spaghetti
- 1 Cup Seasoned Breadcrumbs
- Pinch of Red Pepper Flakes
- 2 Tbs Salt

DIRECTIONS

1. Salt a large pot of water for the spaghetti and bring it to a boil.
2. In a skillet, add olive oil on low heat.
3. Slice the garlic and add to the skillet until golden
4. Add anchovies and a tbs spoon of the oil from the anchovy jar.
5. Once the anchovies start to liquify, add butter, red pepper flakes and wine.
6. Keep on low heat and stir.
7. At this point, the pot of water should be boiling. Cook the spaghetti al dente according to the instructions on the package.
8. Transfer spaghetti with tongs into skillet and add parsley. Mix well. Add a ladle or two of pasta water.
9. Add the breadcrumbs to frying pan and keep pan on low heat until golden brown.
10. Garnish the pasta plates with a sprinkle of toasted breadcrumbs.

Mangia é Statti Zitto!

SPAGHETTI CARBONARA

 SERVES 6-8

Carbonara is a classic Roman dish that is made up of crispy fried pork traditionally using guanciale which is the pork jowl. I have learned to use what I have on hand and at times used pancetta or bacon. The mixture of egg yokes and Pecorino Romano makes the most delicious cream sauce. No cream needed in this recipe. By the time your water boils for the pasta this meal is complete. Such a delicious and quick meal.

INGREDIENTS

1 Pound Spaghetti

4 Eggs

10 oz Guanciale

¾ Cups Pecorino Romano (grated)

2 Tbs Salt

Black Pepper

Pro Tip: Guanciale can be substituted for bacon or pancetta.

DIRECTIONS

1. Salt a large pot of water and bring it to a boil.
2. Cut the guanciale into bite sized pieces and add to the skillet until crispy.
3. Remove guanciale with slotted spoon and set aside.
4. Remove skillet from the heat to cool down.
5. In a medium sized bowl, whisk egg yolks with a couple of pinches of ground pepper.
6. Add the grated cheese to the bowl and mix until thick.
7. Transfer 2-3 tbs of guanciale grease into the egg yolks and whisk.
8. At this point, the water should be boiling. Add the spaghetti and cook al dente according to the package instructions.
9. Heat the skillet again on low heat and transfer spaghetti with tongs into the skillet. Once you add the spaghetti, remove from heat.
10. Pour egg yolk mixture over the spaghetti in the skillet and mix well to coat everything.
11. Add a ladle of the pasta water and continue to mix.
12. Plate the pasta into individual bowls and garnish with guanciale.

Mangia é Statti Zitto!

MEAT

BRACIOLE

 SERVES 4-6

Braciole is a classic Italian American dish often served on Sundays. It is also known as Involtini. This thinly sliced meat is stuffed with fresh parsley, cheese and prosciutto. These rolls are seared and submerged in a rich tomato sauce. The meat becomes so tender and flavorful.

INGREDIENTS

- 2 Flank Steaks
- ½ Pound Prosciutto Di Parma
- ½ Pound Provolone Cheese
- ½ Cup Parmigiano Reggiano
- 5-6 Garlic Cloves
- 2 Cups Seasoned Breadcrumbs
- 1 Handful of Fresh Chopped Parsley
- Black Pepper
- Extra Virgin Olive Oil
- Twine
- 4-6 Cups Marinara Sauce

***Pro Tip:** I like using flank or skirt steaks with this recipe.*

DIRECTIONS

1. Thin out flank steaks with a mallet.
2. If flank steaks are very large, cut in half.
3. Season with black pepper on both sides.
4. In a food processor, mix garlic, breadcrumbs, Parmigiano Reggiano and parsley.
5. Slowly add olive oil to the food processor until you get a paste like consistency.
6. Line each steak with a thin layer of Prosciutto.
7. Using the teeth side of the mallet, push the Prosciutto into the steak.
8. Add a thin layer of the breadcrumb mixture on top of the Prosciutto.
9. Add a thin layer of provolone on top of the breadcrumbs.
10. Roll tight and secure with twine.
11. Add 2-3 tbs of olive oil to a frying pan on medium heat.
12. Once the pan is hot, add the braciole.
13. Fry on all sides until browned.
14. Transfer the braciole into a saucepot with tongs on low heat.
15. Cook in marinara sauce for 1-2 hours.
16. Remove braciole from the saucepot and let cool before removing the twine.
17. Serve whole or sliced over your favorite macaroni or polenta.

Mangia é Statti Zitto!

CHICKEN CACCIATORE

 SERVES 8-10

This is a family style, one-pan rustic meal that is so easy and flavorful. This meal was forever changing due to whatever my Grandma, Nonna Tess, had on hand from the garden. We could always count on this dish being in the weekly rotation.

INGREDIENTS

3-4 Pounds Chicken Legs or Assorted Bone-In Pieces
4 Large Potatoes
2-3 Red Peppers
6-8 Pepperoncini
2 Small Jars Artichoke Hearts
2 Onions
1 Bag Frozen Peas
2 Cans of Whole Peeled Tomatoes
1 Cup Extra Virgin Olive Oil
4 Springs Thyme
4 Springs Rosemary
2 Cups Red Wine
½ Cup Black Cured Olives (pitted)
½ Cup Green Olives (pitted)
6 Garlic Cloves

DIRECTIONS

1. Preheat oven to 400°F.
2. Cut red peppers and onions into slices.
3. Cut potatoes into bite sized pieces.
4. In two baking dishes, spread all ingredients evenly between both. When adding the tomatoes, gently break apart with your hands while pouring.
5. Drizzle the olive oil over both baking dishes.
6. Bake in oven at 400°F for 1 hour or longer if needed.

Mangia é Statti Zitto!

CHICKEN MEATBALLS

 MAKES 27

In my hometown, I am known for this popular dish. Local farm, Raleigh's Poultry Farm, sells my chicken meatballs year-round.

INGREDIENTS

3 Pounds Ground Chicken

6 Garlic Cloves

1 ½ Cups Pecorino Romano Cheese (grated)

½ Loaf Italian Bread

3 Tbs Dried Basil

½ Cup Dried Parsley

2-3 Tbs Fresh Chopped Parsley

½ Tsp Salt

½ Tsp Pepper

2-3 Cups Breadcrumbs

12 oz Marinara Sauce

Extra Virgin Olive Oil

DIRECTIONS

1. Leave bread out overnight to get hard.
2. Soak bread in a large bowl of water until soft.
3. Drain the water using a strainer.
4. Add chicken, cheese, crushed garlic, basil, dried parsley, fresh chopped parsley, salt and pepper to the large bowl with bread.
5. Mix well until all ingredients are incorporated.
6. Place breadcrumbs in a separate bowl.
7. Form chicken mixture into balls and roll in the breadcrumbs.
8. Pour ¼ cup of olive oil into a frying pan on medium to low heat.
9. Once heated, fry all sides of the meatballs in the olive oil. You may need to add additional olive oil as you continue frying.
10. Set the meatballs aside on paper towels to absorb any excess oil.
11. Once all meatballs are fried, serve with marinara sauce.
12. Garnish with extra parsley and grated cheese.

Mangia é Statti Zitto!

CHICKEN PICCATA

 SERVES 6-8

Chicken Piccata is an easy dish. The combination of butter, lemon, capers and wine makes a delicious sauce making the chicken so juicy and flavorful. This meal is requested often in my house.

INGREDIENTS

2 pounds (~8) thin chicken cutlets

2 cups flour

6 garlic cloves

1 jar of capers

3 lemons

4 tbs butter

1 cup white wine

¾ cup extra virgin olive oil

Salt

Pepper

DIRECTIONS

1. Cut the garlic into thin slices and set aside.
2. Season chicken with salt and pepper and set aside.
3. Pour the flour into a bowl.
4. Add 2 tbs of butter and ¼ cup of the olive oil to a frying pan on low heat.
5. Coat each cutlet in flour on both sides.
6. When butter is melted, add the cutlets, 3 cloves of sliced garlic and a tbs of capers to the frying pan.
7. Once garlic starts to brown, add ½ cup of the wine and juice from 1 lemon to the frying pan.
8. Cook for 2-3 minutes before flipping the cutlets for an additional 1-2 minutes.
9. Remove cutlets from the frying pan and place on a platter.
10. Scoop up the juice, garlic and capers and place a little on each cutlet.
11. Serve with extra lemon wedges.

Mangia é Statti Zitto!

EASY WHOLE ROASTED CHICKEN

 SERVES 7-8

INGREDIENTS

7-8 Pound Whole Oven Stuffer
2 Lemons
2 Large Onions
4 Springs Rosemary
4 Springs Thyme
1 Stick Butter
1 Garlic Bulb
1 Cup White Wine
1 Cup Fresh Chopped Parsley
Salt
Pepper
Twine or Skewers

DIRECTIONS

1. Preheat the oven to 350°F.
2. Clean chicken and remove any packet or gizzard from inside the cavity.
3. Pat dry using paper towels.
4. Place chicken in a roasting pan.
5. Season the inside and outside of the chicken with salt and pepper.
6. Carefully season under the skin with salt and pepper.
7. In a saucepan, melt butter and add parsley on low heat until butter is melted.
8. Cut up onions and lemons into slices.
9. Cut the top off the garlic bulb, keeping the bulb intact.
10. Fill the cavity with the garlic bulb, rosemary, thyme and half of the onions and lemons.
11. Place the remaining onions and lemons around the chicken in the roasting pan.
12. Lift the skin and pour the melted butter underneath and on top of the skin.
13. Secure the legs and wings with twine or skewers.
14. Pour the wine into the roasting pan.
15. Cook in oven at 350°F for 20 minutes per pound of chicken.

Mangia é Statti Zitto!

PORK CHOPS WITH CHERRY PEPPERS

 SERVES 4-6

This was Grandma, Nonna Tess's, signature dish. These are the most flavorful and tender pork chops. The secret might just be the adding some of that delicious vinegar from the pepper jar.

INGREDIENTS

4-6 Bone-In Pork Chops

2 Onions

1 Large Jar of Cherry Peppers

1 Large Jar of Roasted Peppers

3 Eggs

4-6 Pepperoncini

3 Cups Seasoned Breadcrumbs

1 Cup Pecorino Romano Cheese (Grated)

Salt

Pepper

Extra Virgin Olive Oil

DIRECTIONS

1. Season both sides of the pork chops with salt and pepper.
2. Prepare two bowls, one with mixed eggs and the other with breadcrumbs and cheese.
3. Coat both sides of the pork chops by dipping into the egg mixture first, then the breadcrumbs and set aside.
4. In a large frying pan, coat the bottom with olive oil on medium heat.
5. Slice the onions and roasted peppers.
6. Add half of the onions, roasted peppers, cherry peppers and pepperoncini into the frying pan on low heat until peppers start to char.
7. Nestle 2-3 pork chops in the frying pan for roughly 3-6 minutes per side. Depending on thickness, pork chops might need an additional 1-2 minutes.
8. For the last few minutes of cooking, add a ½ cup of the vinegar from the cherry pepper jar to the frying pan.
9. Repeat the last 3 steps for the other half of the ingredients.
10. Serve over creamy mashed potatoes or polenta.

Mangia é Statti Zitto!

SAUSAGE WITH ONIONS, FENNEL & GRAPES

 SERVES 8

Enjoy this fabulously rustic dish that would not typically be seen on a menu.

INGREDIENTS

- 1 Bulb Fennel
- 3 Garlic Cloves
- 1 Cup Green Grapes
- 1 Cup Red Grapes
- 2 Pounds Sweet Sausage
- 1 Pound Hot Sausage
- 1 Large Onion
- ¼ Cup Extra Virgin Olive Oil
- ¼ Cup Balsamic Vinegar
- 2-3 Tbs Fresh Chopped Parsley
- Salt
- Pepper

DIRECTIONS

1. Preheat oven to 400°F.
2. In a skillet, sauté sausages until all sides are browned.
3. Transfer to a roasting pan with garlic.
4. In the skillet, add fennel and onions on low heat. Season with salt and pepper and sauté until onions are translucent.
5. Slice the grapes in half and add to skillet with balsamic vinegar, olive oil and parsley.
6. Sauté for an additional 10-12 minutes at low heat.
7. Now pour the skillet mixture into the roasting pan with the sausages.
8. Bake for 30-40 minutes.

Pro Tips: *This meal is delicious over mashed potatoes or polenta. The sausages can be kept as links or sliced before adding to the skillet.*

Mangia é Statti Zitto!

STEAK PIZZAIOLA

 SERVES 6-8

A generational meal from my maternal grandma, Nonna Matteo.

INGREDIENTS

Two 2-Pound Pieces of Chuck Steak
Koscher Salt
Black Pepper
1 Large Onion
1 Cup Red Wine
Red Pepper Flakes
2-3 Garlic Cloves
2-3 Tbs Extra Virgin Olive Oil
2 Cans Crushed Tomatoes
Handful of Fresh Chopped Parsley

DIRECTIONS

1. Season steaks on both sides with salt and pepper.
2. Pour olive oil in a skillet on medium heat.
3. Once pan is hot, add the steaks and sear for 5 minutes on each side.
4. Chop up the onions.
5. Flip the steak and add chopped onions, garlic cloves and a pinch of red pepper flakes.
6. Once onions brown and garlic is golden, reduce to low heat and add crushed tomatoes, wine and parsley.
7. Cover with a lid or foil and keep on low heat for 2-3 hours.
8. Stir occasionally.
9. The meal is ready when the steak is fork tender.
10. Serve over favorite pasta, potatoes or polenta.

Mangia é Statti Zitto!

STUFFED CHICKEN CUTLETS

 SERVES 2-4

INGREDIENTS

1 Pound Chicken Cutlets

2 Cups Seasoned Breadcrumbs

Scamorza

1 Pound Prosciutto Di Parma

Black Pepper

½ Cup Extra Virgin Olive Oil

2 Cups Fresh Baby Spinach

DIRECTIONS

1. Preheat oven to 375°F.
2. Wash and pat dry your cutlets.
3. Drizzle baking sheet with just enough oil to coat the bottom.
4. Place breadcrumbs in a bowl.
5. Coat each cutlet front and back with breadcrumbs and place on the baking sheet.
6. Place 1 piece of Prosciutto on each cutlet followed by a ¼ cup of shredded or grated scamorza and ½ cup of baby spinach.
7. Roll the cutlets and place seam side down.
8. Add a drizzle of olive oil on top to keep moist.
9. Bake at 375°F for 20-25 minutes.
10. Serve whole or make slices for a beautiful presentation.

Mangia é Statti Zitto!

TRIPE

 SERVES 4-6

Tripe is another dish I grew up on. My Grandfather Modestino loved this dish and made it often. Living next to my paternal grandparents, I was introduced to different foods that my friends weren't accustomed to. It's important to me to pass down these generational recipes to my kids. I'm happy to expose them to different foods. Tripe is not the most popular dish these days because people are nervous to try or had a bad experience. If the tripe is undercooked, it can be extremely rubbery. The longer it cooks, the more tender it will become.

INGREDIENTS

2 Pounds Tripe
1 Onion
Extra Virgin Olive Oil
Salt
2-3 Cups Marinara Sauce

DIRECTIONS

1. Clean and soak the tripe in cold water for 5-10 minutes.
2. Slice the onion and add with the tripe to a large pot of salted water. Bring to a boil.
3. Keep the pot covered and cook for 2 ½ hours or until tripe is completely tender.
4. If making marinara sauce, prepare while the tripe is cooking.
5. Remove tripe with tongs and place in individual bowls.
6. Cover tripe with marinara sauce.

Mangia é Statti Zitto!

FISH

BAKED CLAMS

 SERVES 36

A true classic appetizer for birthdays and holidays. A family favorite!

INGREDIENTS

2 Dozen Little Neck Clams
1 Large Onion
½ Pound Bacon
1 Cup Pecorino Romano (Grated)
1 Beer (IPA)
1 Cup White Wine
3 Garlic Cloves
1 Cup Seasoned Breadcrumbs
3 Tbs Butter
1 Lemon
1 Cup Fresh Chopped Parsley
Pepper
2 Cans Chopped Clams (optional)

DIRECTIONS

1. Preheat oven to 350°F.
2. Wash and clean clams in a strainer.
3. Add clams to a deep skillet with wine, beer and lemon wedges.
4. Simmer on medium-low heat until clams start to pop open.
5. Remove clams from skillet with slotted spoon as soon as they open.
6. Once cooled, chop up the clams and set aside.
7. Cut up bacon into bite size pieces and fry in a separate pan.
8. Once bacon starts to slightly crisp up, add chopped onion.
9. Sauté until the onions turn translucent.
10. Keep on low heat and add butter, minced garlic, pepper, breadcrumbs, cheese, clams and parsley.
11. You can add a can or two of chopped clams at this point if you desire more clams.
12. Sauté on low 2-3 minutes.
13. Stuff clam shells with filling.
14. Place on cookie sheet and bake for 10-12 minutes at 350°F.

Mangia é Statti Zitto!

BRONZINO

 SERVES 4-6

A great dish to make during Lent. It's a quarter of the price to make it at home vs at a restaurant. My kids love it and taking my family of 7 out to dinner can be costly so I decided to perfect this at home for the whole family to enjoy.

INGREDIENTS

Parchment Paper
2 Bronzino gutted and cleaned
2 Onions
3 Lemons
1 Red Onion
2 Cups Cherry Tomatoes
2 Potatoes
1 Bunch Asparagus
Black Pepper
Salt
3 Cloves Garlic
1 Handful Fresh Chopped Parsley
Extra Virgin Olive Oil

DIRECTIONS

1. Preheat oven to 350°F.
2. Line a baking sheet with the parchment paper.
3. Score each side of the Bronzino three times 2 inches apart.
4. Lay out 3 slices of lemon under each fish on the sheet.
5. Now stuff the remainder of the sliced lemons and thick sliced onions into each fish.
6. Slice the cherry tomatoes in half and spread out on the sheet.
7. Add the asparagus onto one side of the sheet.
8. Peel and slice the potatoes and spread onto the sheet.
9. Place the garlic on the sheet.
10. Slice the onions and spread on the sheet.
11. Drizzle the olive oil and parsley on top with a pinch of salt and pepper.
12. Bake for 20-25 minutes at 350°F.

Mangia é Statti Zitto!

COD PUTTANESCA

 SERVES 4-6

A creative variation for a cod fish recipe that is typically served on the table for the Feast of the Seven Fishes. A staple growing up with my Dad.

INGREDIENTS

¼ Cup Extra Virgin Olive Oil

1 Cup Mixed Olives (Black Cured, Kalamata and Sicilian Green)

3 Cloves Garlic

3 Tbs Capers

3-4 Anchovy Fillets (from a jar)

1 Can Whole Peeled Tomatoes

2-3 Tbs Fresh Chopped Parsley

Pinch Red Pepper Flakes

2 Cups All Purpose Flour

Salt

Pepper

½ Cup White Wine

2 Large Cod

Pro Tip: *Omit the flour to make this dish gluten free.*

DIRECTIONS

1. Add olive oil and garlic to a skillet. Sauté on low until garlic is browned.
2. Keep the skillet on low heat during these next steps.
3. Add the anchovies into the skillet.
4. Measure out a tbs of the oil inside the anchovy jar and add to the skillet.
5. Add red pepper flakes.
6. Using a wooden spoon, mix the anchovies until they dissolve.
7. Break tomatoes apart by hand before adding them to the skillet.
8. Chop up the olives and add to the skillet with capers.
9. Lastly, add fresh parsley.
10. Keep on low heat while prepping the fish.
11. Wash and pat dry the cod.
12. Lightly season with salt and pepper and cut into equal portions.
13. Take each chunk of fish and dredge in flour on both sides.
14. Nestle the pieces of cod into the sauce and simmer on low heat for 7-8 minutes.
15. If the cod is thicker, increase cooking time an additional 5-6 minutes.

Mangia é Statti Zitto!

GRILLED POLPO

 SERVES 6-8

I always look forward to making this with my brother Rocco. We enjoy cooking this over the summer and always on Christmas Eve as part of our Feast of the Seven Fishes.

INGREDIENTS

- 5-7 lbs Octopus
- 2 Cups Black Pepper Corns
- 2 Wine Corks
- 2 Lemons
- ½ Cup Fresh Chopped Parsley
- Extra Virgin Olive Oil

Pro Tip: *The natural enzymes in the corks help to tenderize the octopus*

DIRECTIONS

1. Wash the octopus in a large pan under running water and remove the beak by cutting around it.
2. Fill large lobster pot with water and add peppercorn and corks.
3. Bring to a boil.
4. Dip the octopus half way three separate times for three seconds each. The legs should be curling up.
5. Now slowly submerge octopus into the pot and keep covered for an hour on low heat.
6. Octopus should be fork tender at this point. If not, keep in for additional 10-15 minutes.
7. Remove from pot and place in a pan before coating with olive oil.
8. Grill on medium heat for 2-3 minutes per side or until grill marks start to show.
9. Place octopus on a platter and garnish with lemon wedges and parsley.

Mangia é Statti Zitto!

INSALATA DI MARE

 SERVES 12-18

This is a great seafood salad anytime of the year, especially on Christmas Eve, as one of the Seven Fishes. I like to use the same skillet to get the combination of all the fish flavors in one skillet. I find it easier and more efficient not using so many pots and pans. I like to cook the fish in batches, since there are different cooking times for each fish.

INGREDIENTS

- 1 Pound Calamari Tubes with Tentacles
- 1 Pound Large Shrimp
- 3 Lobster Tails (Approx. 4 oz each)
- 2 Large Lemons (Quartered)
- 1 Tbs Black Peppercorns
- 1 Cup Celery
- 1 Red Onion (Diced)
- 1 Garlic Clove
- 2 Marinated Roasted Peppers
- ½ Cup Fresh Chopped Parsley
- ½ Cup Extra Virgin Olive Oil
- 2-3 Cups Water
- 2 Tbs Butter

DIRECTIONS

1. Wash all seafood.
2. To prepare the lobster, remove lobster meat from shells and cut into bite sized pieces.
3. Keep shells and set aside.
4. To prepare the shrimp, peel and devein shrimp and discard shells and tails.
5. Next, clean calamari tubes, and pull out the tentacles and cartilage. Cartilage feels like hard plastic, discard that.
6. Make slices or rings with calamari tubes and cut the tentacles in half if they are large.
7. Once seafood is all clean, place on paper towels and pat dry.
8. In a deep skillet, add butter, 4 lemon wedges and peppercorns on low heat.
9. Once butter is melted, add water and bring to a simmer.
10. Start by adding Calamari rings and tentacles to skillet and cook on medium heat for 2 minutes.
11. Remove with slotted spoon and add to large bowl.
12. Next, add the shrimp and cook 2-3 minutes.
13. Again, remove with slotted spoon and add to bowl.
14. Add lobster shells and let simmer for 2 to 3 minutes. This will ensure the removal of any bits of meat left inside your lobster shells and will add flavor.
15. Remove the shells and add chopped lobster meat.
16. Cook 2-3 minutes before removing with slotted spoon and adding to a bowl.
17. Lastly, add chopped celery, minced garlic and chopped peppers.
18. Mix well and add 4 lemon wedges.
19. Drizzle extra virgin olive oil on top and add your chopped parsley.
20. Mix well and place in refrigerator or serve warm.

Mangia é Statti Zitto!

MUSSELS MARINARA

 SERVES 12-14

INGREDIENTS

5 Pounds of Mussels
2 Can Whole Peeled Tomatoes
½ Cup Fresh Chopped Parsley
½ Cup White Wine
Red Pepper Flakes
2-3 Cloves Garlic
Extra Virgin Olive Oil
Salt
Pepper

Pro Tip: I like to save the sauce for pasta! It will last up to 5 days in the fridge

DIRECTIONS

1. Soak the mussels in a large bowl of cool water with 2 tbs of salt. This will slightly open the mussels just enough to loosen the beards to easily be removed.
2. De-beard by holding the mussel in one hand and using your opposite hands thumb and forefinger to grip the beard, pulling down towards the bottom of the shell. Using a cloth to grab the beard can assist in this process.
3. Using a butter knife, remove any barnacles attached to the shells.
4. Lay the mussels all out on a dish towel and pat dry with paper towels.
5. In a deep skillet, add 2-3 tbs of olive oil and garlic and sauté about 5 minutes until garlic is golden.
6. Add a few pinches of red pepper flakes and mix gently with a wooden spoon.
7. Now, pour in the tomatoes while gently breaking them apart with your hand.
8. Pour the white wine and simmer for 15 minutes on low.
9. Add the mussels into the skillet all at once and cover with heavy lid or sheet pan and continue to simmer for about 8-10 minutes.
10. Remove the mussels with a slotted spoon as they pop open.
11. Garnish with parsley.

Mangia é Statti Zitto!

SHRIMP OREGANATA

 SERVES 8-10

Here's a quick, super easy and delicious shrimp dish to add to your Christmas menu. I promise you this mixture of buttery garlic & breadcrumbs is delicious! The feast of the seven fishes represents the seven sacraments in the Catholic Church. Although most years we definitely have more than seven fish on Christmas Eve, it is definitely one of my most favorite traditions.

INGREDIENTS

- 2 Pounds Shrimp
- Extra Virgin Olive Oil
- 1 Cup Italian Seasoned Breadcrumbs
- ¼ Cup Parmigiano Reggiano Cheese (Grated)
- 2 Cloves Garlic
- 2 Tbs Butter
- 3 Tbs Fresh Chopped Parsley
- 1 Lemon

DIRECTIONS

1. Preheat oven to 350°F.
2. First, make sure the shrimp are cleaned and de-veined.
3. Once clean, pat the shrimp down with a paper towel to dry them.
4. Coat a pan with olive oil before adding the shrimp to the pan.
5. Sprinkle breadcrumbs on top with grated cheese, crushed garlic, butter and fresh chopped parsley.
6. Mix and bake in the oven at 350°F for 10 minutes.
7. Serve with lemon wedges.

Mangia é Statti Zitto!

STUFFED CALAMARI

 SERVES 6

A true Christmas Eve tradition. For as early as I can remember, I helped my Dad stuff the calamari.

INGREDIENTS

- ½ Pound Calamari Tubes with Tentacles
- 3 Anchovy Fillets
- 7 Cloves Garlic
- 2 Cups Seasoned Breadcrumbs
- 1 Can Fresh Lump Crab Meat
- ½ Cup Grated Pecorino Romano
- ¼ Cup Fresh Chopped Parsley
- 4 Tbs Melted Butter
- ¼ Cup White Wine
- ½ Cup Chicken Broth
- 2 Cans Crushed Tomatoes
- ½ Cup Red Wine
- Toothpicks
- Black Pepper
- Red Pepper Flakes
- Extra Virgin Olive Oil

DIRECTIONS

1. In a large pot, coat the bottom with olive oil and add 3 cloves of garlic.
2. Sauté on low until garlic is golden and add 1-2 pinches of red pepper flakes.
3. Add the crushed tomatoes, red wine and cover the pot to simmer on low for 20 minutes.
4. For the Calamari, start by cleaning the tubes. Remove the hard cartilage (feels like hard plastic) inside the tubes and discard.
5. Remove tentacles and chop them up into bite sized pieces.
6. In a large bowl, add tentacles, breadcrumbs, cheese, parsley, anchovies, melted butter, crab meat and 4 cloves of crushed garlic.
7. Mix together and slowly add the white wine.
8. Lastly add the chicken broth. Mix well.
9. Stuff the tubes and secure them with a toothpick.
10. Add the tubes to the sauce pot and cook on low heat for 30 minutes.
11. This can be served whole or sliced.

Pro Tip: If the stuffing seems dry, keep adding in a tbs of chicken broth until you get a wet sand consistency. You can fill the tubes by hand or it can be easier to use a pastry bag.

Mangia é Statti Zitto!

STUFFED FLOUNDER

 SERVES 6

INGREDIENTS

6 Flounder Fillets
3 Cups Seasoned Breadcrumbs
3 Cups Fresh Lump Crabmeat
1 Cup Grated Parmigiano Reggiano
½ Cup Fresh Chopped Parsley
½ Cup Vegetable Broth
2 Lemon
3 Cloves Garlic
12 Tbs Butter
1 Cup White Wine
2 Tbs Extra Virgin Olive Oil
Paprika

DIRECTIONS

1. Preheat oven to 350°F.
2. In a large bowl, add breadcrumbs, crabmeat, grated cheese, parsley, ½ cup of the white wine, juice from one lemon and softened butter.
3. Mix all of these together.
4. Now coat the baking dish with olive oil.
5. Lay the flounder out and stuff each one with ½ cup to 1 cup of filling each.
6. Roll each flounder tight and place in the baking dish with the seam side down.
7. Pour the other ½ cup of white wine in the dish.
8. Place 1 tbs of butter along with a lemon slice on each flounder.
9. Place in oven for 30 minutes at 350°F.
10. Garnish with any leftover parsley and sprinkle with paprika.

Mangia é Statti Zitto!

DESSERTS

ITALIAN CHEESECAKE

 SERVES 8-10

A delicious cheesecake that my family counts on me to make every year at Easter. I love that this has no crust which helps focus on the pure creaminess of the cheesecake.

INGREDIENTS

3 Pounds Whole Milk Ricotta
8 Eggs
2 Tsp Vanilla Extract
1 Orange
1 Lemon
1 ½ Cups Sugar
¾ Cup Corn Starch
1 Tbs Butter
1 Tsp Flour
9" Springform Pan
Roasting Pan
Aluminum Foil

DIRECTIONS

1. Preheat oven to 350°F.
2. Place springform pan on a 12" square sheet of aluminum foil. Mold foil tightly around pan to seal bottom edge. This will prevent water seeping into the pan in a later step.
3. Mix ricotta until smooth before adding vanilla and eggs one at a time. Mix until well blended.
4. In a separate bowl, stir together sugar and cornstarch before adding to the ricotta mixture.
5. Grate 1 tbs of both orange and lemon peel and add to the mixture.
6. Place springform pan into a roasting pan. Grease and dust springform pan with butter and flour.
7. Pour mixture into the springform pan.
8. Pour hot water into roasting pan until it's 1 inch deep.
9. Bake in oven on middle rack for 1 ½ hours. Test doneness with a butter knife. If the knife comes out clean, move on to the next step. If not, keep in oven and retest at 5 minute intervals.
10. Before removing from the oven, turn oven off and let sit for an additional 30 minutes.
11. Remove and let cool before serving.

Mangia é Statti Zitto!

GRAIN PIE

 SERVES 8

As a child, I never really cared for grain pie. It was typically served after dinner on Easter. I have grown to really enjoy this dessert. My maternal grandma, Nonna Matteo, would always make a version of this pie. I have added to this recipe to make it both sweeter and creamier. I hope you enjoy it as much as my family! **If on Long Island, visit Italian street market in Lynbrook for the Grano Cotto.**

INGREDIENTS

- 1 Lemon
- 1 Orange
- 580g (20 oz) Italian Grain Grano Cotto
- 2 Pie Crusts
- 2 Cups Whole Milk
- 1 ½ Pounds Whole Milk Ricotta
- 1 Tbs Vanilla Extract
- ¼ Tsp Cinnamon
- 4 Whole Eggs
- 3 Tbs Sugar
- 1 Tsp Salt
- 2 Tbs Butter
- Powdered Sugar

DIRECTIONS

1. Preheat oven to 375°F.
2. In a large pot, add the grain, milk, salt, 1 tbs of butter, 2 lemon peel slices, 2 orange peel slices and sugar.
3. Let simmer for 15 minutes and stir with a wooden spoon until you see a white film start to appear on the bottom of the pot.
4. Remove from heat and extract the peel slices from the pot.
5. In a separate bowl, add the Ricotta, vanilla extract, cinnamon and 3 eggs. Mix well.
6. Gently mix in a little lemon and orange zest. About a tsp each.
7. Now grease a pie plate with the other tbs of butter and place one pie crust on the plate.
8. Transfer the contents of the pot into the bowl and mix will.
9. Pour onto the pie crust.
10. Now set the second pie crust on a cutting board and use a pizza cutter or sharp pairing knife to make strips.
11. Weave the pie crust strips over and under making a lattice on top of the pie crust.
12. Bake for 45 minutes at 375°F.
13. Beat the last egg to make an egg wash.
14. Remove the pie from the oven and brush the egg wash over the lattice being careful to only apply to the crust.
15. Now bake for an additional 15 minutes.
16. Remove and let the pie cool completely before dusting with the powdered sugar.

Mangia é Statti Zitto!

ITALIAN RAINBOW COOKIES

 MAKES 2 DOZEN

INGREDIENTS

6 Eggs (Leave in room temperature for 3 hours beforehand)

3 Sticks Salted Butter

1 Tbs Almond Paste

¾ Cup Sugar

1 Tbs Almond Extract

1 Cup All Purpose Flour

1 Tbs Baking Powder

½ Tsp Vegetable Oil

Green Food Coloring

Red Food Coloring

3 Cups Apricot, Strawberry or Raspberry Preserves

1 Cup Semi-Sweet Chocolate Chips

Non-Stick Baking Spray

3 Aluminum Foil Pans (11 ¾" X 9 ¼")

Pro Tips: Use a measuring cup to separate the mixture into the bowls evenly. Another layer of melted chocolate can be applied to the other side of the cake after refrigerating and before cutting. If you opt for this, place back in the refrigerator for another 20 minutes.

DIRECTIONS

1. Preheat oven to 350°F.
2. Mix the butter and sugar together in the mixer at low speed until blended.
3. Add in oil and eggs one at a time while slowly mixing.
4. Add in almond extract.
5. Mix together at low speed for one minute.
6. In a separate bowl, mix flour and baking powder.
7. Add flour mixture to butter mixture a little at a time.
8. Mix everything together at low speed for two minutes.
9. Separate the mixture evenly into three bowls.
10. In one bowl, mix 4-5 drops of green food coloring. In another bowl, mix 4-5 drops of red food coloring. The third bowl has no food coloring.
11. Spray each pan with baking spray and pour each bowl into a separate pan.
12. Bake at 350°F for 10-12 minutes.
13. Set aside until pans are cool to the touch.
14. Place a large piece of parchment paper down on a cutting board.
15. Flip the pan with the red layer down on the paper first.
16. Spread thin layer of preserves on top of red layer.
17. Now flip the plain layer down on top of the red layer and spread another thin layer of preserves.
18. Finally flip the green layer down on top of the plain layer.
19. Melt chocolate chips in glass bowl in the microwave at 20 second intervals until you have a smooth consistency.
20. Pour the melted chocolate on top of the green layer and spread evenly.
21. Place in refrigerator for 30 minutes to let the chocolate harden.
22. Let sit in room temperature for 10 minutes before cutting and serving.

Mangia é Statti Zitto!

LEMON RICOTTA CAKE

 SERVES 8-10

INGREDIENTS

- ¾ Cup Salted Butter (Plus 1 Tbs for greasing pan)
- 1 ½ Cups Sugar
- 15 oz Whole Milk Ricotta
- 4 Eggs
- 1 Tsp Vanilla Extract
- 2 Lemons
- ½ Tsp Baking Soda
- ½ Tsp Salt
- 1 ½ Cups All Purpose Flour (Plus 1 Tsp for dusting the pan)

DIRECTIONS

1. Preheat oven to 350°F.
2. Whisk softened butter and sugar together in mixer.
3. Add in ricotta and then the eggs one at a time.
4. Once the mixture is smooth, add in the vanilla, lemon juice from two lemons and zest from one lemon.
5. In a separate bowl, mix baking soda and flour together.
6. Slowly add to ricotta mixture.
7. Mix for 2-3 minutes at a low speed.
8. Grease and dust pan with the leftover butter and flour.
9. Pour batter into pan.
10. Bake at 350°F for 50-60 minutes.
11. Let cool for 15 minutes before serving.

Pro Tips: A silicone spatula aids in pouring the mixture into the pan. Soften the butter by leaving out for about an hour or until room temperature.

Mangia é Statti Zitto!

PIGNOLI COOKIES

 MAKES 30

This is a delicious family recipe from my maternal grandma. It also happens to be my personal favorite cookie.

INGREDIENTS

16 oz Almond Paste
2 Egg Whites
1 Pound Pignoli Nuts
1 Cup Sugar
3 Tbs Confection Sugar

DIRECTIONS

1. Preheat oven to 350°F.
2. Whisk the almond paste and sugar together.
3. Add egg whites and whisk for about 3 minutes.
4. Pour pignoli nuts into a bowl.
5. Line a cookie sheet with parchment paper.
6. Keep hands damp for the next few steps.
7. Using a tablespoon, scoop out the mixture and roll into a ball with your hands.
8. Roll each ball in the pignoli nuts before placing on parchment paper.
9. Using the bottom of a glass, gently flatten each ball.
10. Bake for 10-12 minutes.
11. If you decided to make bigger cookies, add 2-4 minutes to the baking time.
12. Remove cookies and let cool before dusting with confection sugar.

Mangia é Statti Zitto!

RICE PUDDING

 SERVES 4-6

While this isn't traditionally a dessert that kids ask for, my version is sweeter and creamier. The amaretto gives tremendous flavor sure to impress all who try it.

INGREDIENTS

1 Cup Raisins
½ Cup Amaretto
2 Tbs Butter
2 Cups Arborio Rice
1 Tsp Vanilla Extract
8 Cups Of Heavy Or Light Cream
1 Cup Sugar
2 Eggs
Ground Cinnamon

DIRECTIONS

1. Soak raisins in amaretto in a shallow dish for at least 60 minutes or overnight.
2. In a large saucepan, add cream, ½ cup of sugar and vanilla on low heat for 2-3 minutes. Whisk for sugar to dissolve.
3. Melt butter in a skillet on medium heat.
4. Add rice all at once to the skillet.
5. Mix with a wooden spoon until rice is slightly toasted.
6. Turn heat to low and add half of the cream one ladle at a time.
7. Using a double broiler, add egg yolks and the other ½ cup of sugar on low heat.
8. Whisk until you get a custard-like consistency.
9. If you do not have a double broiler, use a glass bowl over a saucepan of boiling water.
10. Slowly add the custard to the skillet.
11. Continue adding the cream one ladle at a time until the rice is plump and tender.
12. Add the raisins and mix well.
13. Remove from heat and place in a serving dish.
14. Sprinkle with cinnamon.

Mangia é Statti Zitto!

SICILIAN ORANGE CAKE

 SERVES 8-10

My maternal Grandmother loved this cake. This was another delicious recipe that was passed down. Unfortunately I did not have the full recipe but with a little trial and error I was able to recreate a perfectly comparable version. It is so fresh, delicious and made of 8 simple ingredients.

INGREDIENTS

1 ⅔ Cups All Purpose Flour
1 Cup Almond Flour
3 Eggs
¾ Cup Sugar
3 Tbs Powdered Sugar
1 Tbs Baking Powder
3 Whole Oranges
10 ½ Tbs Unsalted Butter
    (Plus ½ Tbs For Greasing Pan)
9" Springform Pan

DIRECTIONS

1. Preheat oven to 355°F.
2. Cut 2 oranges into quarters (with peel) and put in blender.
3. Mix eggs and sugar until fluffy and white.
4. Add blended oranges into the egg mixture.
5. Melt butter, add to egg mixture and mix gently.
6. In a separate bowl, mix baking powder and flour.
7. Sift this mixture gently into egg bowl.
8. Add in almond flour.
9. Butter a springform pan with leftover butter.
10. Pour batter into the pan and bake for 30-40 minutes.
11. While baking batter, start making the glaze.
12. Squeeze juice of one orange into a bowl and add the powdered sugar. Whisk gently.
13. Once cake is cooled, add glaze on top.

Mangia é Statti Zitto!

TIRAMISU

 SERVES 16

Tiramisu is a classic Italian dessert. This is made of airy ladyfingers dipped in espresso and covered with layers of a delicious cream filling. You will love this no bake dessert.

INGREDIENTS

36 Savoiardi Cookies (Lady Fingers)
1 Tbs Vanilla Extract
2 Cups Espresso
4 Large Eggs
½ Cup Sugar
4 Tbs Mascarpone
2 Tbs Cocoa Powder
1 Packet Paneangeli Vanillina (optional)
10" X 10" Baking Dish

DIRECTIONS

1. Make 2 cups of espresso with your preferred method.
2. Let cool and pour into baking dish with vanilla extract.
3. Separate your eggs into two separate bowls. One for egg whites and one for yolks.
4. Add two cups of water to a saucepan and bring to a boil.
5. Place the bowl of egg yolks on top of sauce pan and whisk until you have a custard like consistency while slowly adding sugar.
6. Remove the egg yolk bowl from sauce pan and set aside.
7. Add packet of Vanillina to the egg white bowl and whisk at medium speed for 2-3 minutes or until stiff peaks form. The egg whites should be thick enough for you to turn the bowl upside down.
8. Add mascarpone to egg yolk bowl and whisk gently while adding egg white mix a little at a time using a spatula to fold over.
9. Dunk each cookie into the espresso quickly coating each side. If allowed to dwell too long in the espresso, the cookie will get soggy.
10. Line baking dish with a single layer of cookies (18) touching side by side.
11. Put a thick layer of cream mixture on top of cookies.
12. Dust half the cocoa powder on top of the cream.
13. Add a second layer of cookies (18) on top.
14. Place the rest of the cream on top of the second layer of cookies and cover.
15. Place in refrigerator for a minimum of 3 hours.
16. Before serving, dust the other half of the cocoa powder covering the entire sheet.

Mangia é Statti Zitto!

Italian/American
WORDS & PHRASES

Growing up in an Italian / American household certain words and phrases were often used and part of our everyday life. Whether it was food, slang, affectionate or not-so affectionate nicknames. Here are just a few I heard all the time. Maybe you'll recognize some.

Mangia e'Statti Zitto	*Eat n Shut Up*
Goombah (Goom-bah)	*Friend*
Mamaluke (mama-luke)	*Idiot*
Fugazi (foo-GAH-zee)	*Fake*
Agita (ah-jee-tah)	*Aggravation / heartburn*
Oogatz (oo-gatz)	*Nothing/ you got nothing*
Mooshad (Moo-shad)	*Mushy*
Mapine (Ma-peen)	*Dish towel*
Faccia Brutta (Faa-chuh-broot)	*Ugly face*
Goomah/ Goomad (Goo-MAAD)	*Mistress*
Medigan (Meh-dee-gan)	*Someone who is not italian/ American people*
Skivats (skee-vatz)	*Disgusting*
Doozy Batz (doo-zee-batz)	*Crazy*
Mannaggia (Maa-Naa-jah)	*Damn*
Stunud (stoo-nad)	*Stupid*
Chooch (choo-ch)	*Idiot*
Sculabast (school-AH-BAAST)	*Strainer/ colander*
Bachagaloop (Bah-cha-gah-loop)	*Dummy*
Proshoot (pro-shoo- toh)	*Prosciutto*
Galamad (gah- lah- mahd)	*Calamari*

Acknowledgments

I would like to express my heartfelt gratitude to everyone who helped bring this cookbook to life. This project would not have been possible without the foundation laid by my parents, Rocco and Joanne, and grandparents, whose love, traditions, and passion for food have deeply inspired me.

I thank God every day for the incredible family I was born into, including my three amazing older brothers Joseph, Rocco and Brian. My appreciation extends to my husband Patrick, and our five beautiful children, my stepparents Andy and Arlene, my Godmother Connie, all my wonderful nieces and nephews, uncles, aunts, sister-in-laws, in-laws Pat and Cathy, cousins, and all my dear friends who have become like family to us.

To my daughter Rosalie and good friend Joe Sardo—thank you for encouraging me to start an Instagram account, a step that helped set this entire journey in motion.

A special thank you to:

- Allison, Second Oak Designs, @second_oak
- Casa Della Mozzarella on Arthur Ave, Bronx, @casadellamozzarella
- Dena Fenza, @miciamammas
- Derek Ciliotta, @keepersonlyco, keepersonlyco.com
- Joe Caporaso with Remember Yesteryears in Oakdale, Ny, @Ny_hidden_treasures
- Kristy Twellmann, for the beautiful book design, @umbrellasquared
- Ken Hild, for the stunning photography, @kenhildphotography
- Lisa Marie, for hair and makeup, @m1ssl1samar1e
- Maia Salon + Spa, @maiasalon
- Nest On Main, @nestonmainmarket
- Nicolas Cassio and George Regini, from Giorgio's Caterers, @giorgiosvatinghollow
- "Nono" Vincenzo, at the Italian Street Market in Lynbrook, @italianstreetmarketlynbrook
- Rocco Caporaso owner of Gliptone, Inc. Ronkonkoma, Ny, @gliptone_usa, www.gliptone.com
- Ruggiero family, from Raleigh's Farm
- Salpino Italian Food Market in North Bellmore, @salpinofoodmarket
- Samantha Caporaso, @caporaso_custom_creations
- Santoro's Italian Deli, @santoroitaliandeli
- Teitel Brothers on Arthur Ave in the Bronx, @teitelbrotherssince1915
- Tom Ciliotta, Old Country Ceramic Tile, Westbury & Port Jeff Station, @oldcountrytile

Your support, talent, and generosity have helped shape this cookbook into something truly special. I will cherish your contributions always.

INDEX

A

Almond Flour
- Sicilian Orange Cake 173

Almond Paste
- Italian Rainbow Cookies 165
- Pignoli Cookies 169

Amaretto
- Rice Pudding 171

Artichoke Hearts
- Chicken Cacciatore 121
- Chicken Piccata 125
- Spinach Artichoke Dip 55

Asparagus
- Asparagus with Béchamel Sauce 71
- Bronzino 143
- Cream of Asparagus Soup 19

B

Bacon
- Baked Clams 141
- Clam Chowder 17
- Creamy Broccoli Soup 21
- Creamy Potato Soup 23
- Spinach Artichoke Dip 55

Baking Powder
- Italian Rainbow Cookies 165
- Sicilian Orange Cake 173

Balsamic Glaze
- Fried Burrata Bombs 45

Balsamic Vinegar
- Sausage with Onions, Fennel & Grapes 131

Beer
- Baked Clams 141
- Linguine & Clams 101

Bread
- Italian Bread
  - Burrata with Roasted Tomatoes & Garlic 37
  - Chicken Meatballs 123
  - Stuffed Cabbage 83
  - Stuffed Meatballs 61
- Provolone Bread
  - Burrata with Roasted Tomatoes & Garlic 37
- White Bread
  - Mozzarella in Carrozza 47
  - Stuffed Cabbage 83

Breadcrumbs
- Arancini 69
- Chicken Meatballs 123
- Gnudi 97
- Panko Breadcrumbs
  - Stuffed & Fried Sicilian Olives 57
- Seasoned Breadcrumbs
  - Baked Clams 141
  - Braciole 119
  - Calamari Oreganata 39
  - Eggplant Rollatini 43
  - Fried Burrata Bombs 45
  - Mozzarella in Carrozza 47
  - Pork Chops with Cherry Peppers 129
  - Shrimp Oreganata 153
  - Sicilian Style Stuffed Peppers 53
  - Spaghetti Aglio e Alici 113
  - Stuffed Artichokes 81
  - Stuffed Calamari 155
  - Stuffed Cherry Peppers 59
  - Stuffed Chicken Cutlets 135
  - Stuffed Flounder 157
  - Stuffed Meatballs 61
  - Stuffed Mushrooms 63
  - Stuffed Peppers & Rice 65
- Suppli 85

Broccoli
- Creamy Broccoli Soup 21

Broccoli, Rabe
- Broccoli Rabe with Sausage & Orecchiette 91

Butter
- Asparagus with Béchamel Sauce 71
- Cream of Asparagus Soup 19
- Easy Whole Roasted Chicken 127
- Gnocchi 95
- Gnudi 97
- Insalata di Mare 149
- Italian Cheesecake 161
- Italian Rainbow Cookies 165
- Lemon Ricotta Cake 167
- Linguine & Clams 101

Lobster & Shrimp Fra Diavolo 103
Mozzarella in Carrozza 47
Pan Seared Scallops 49
Polenta 73
Rice Pudding 171
Roasted Butternut Squash Soup 33
Sauteed Cabbage with Pancetta 79
Scallops Saltimbocca 51
Shrimp Oreganata 153
Sicilian Orange Cake 173
Spaghetti Aglio e Alici 113
Stuffed Calamari 155
Stuffed Cherry Peppers 59
Stuffed Flounder 157
Stuffed Mushrooms 63

C

Calamari
- Calamari Oreganata 39
- Insalata di Mare 149
- Stuffed Calamari 155

Capers
- Cod Puttanesca 145
- Puttanesca 109

Carrots
- Lentil Soup 29
- Roasted Butternut Squash Soup 33
- Stuffed Cabbage 83
- Stuffed & Fried Sicilian Olives 57

Celery
- Clam Chowder 17
- Insalata di Mare 149
- Lentil Soup 29
- Stuffed & Fried Sicilian Olives 57

Cheddar
- Creamy Broccoli Soup 21

Creamy Potato Soup 23

Cheese
- Cheddar
  - Creamy Broccoli Soup 21
  - Creamy Potato Soup 23
- Cream Cheese
  - Spinach Artichoke Dip 55
- Goat Cheese
  - Creamy Asparagus Soup 19
- Mascarpone
  - Tiramisu 175
- Mozzarella
  - Aunt Concetta's Manicotti 89
  - Eggplant Rollatini 43
  - Lasagna 99
  - Mozzarella in Carrozza 47
  - Stuffed Meatballs 61
  - Suppli 85
- Parmigiano Romano
  - Polenta 73
- Pecorino Romano
  - Arancini 69
  - Aunt Concetta's Manicotti 89
  - Baked Clams 141
  - Calamari Oreganata 39
  - Chicken Meatballs 123
  - Eggplant Rollatini 43
  - Escarole & Beans with Sausage Orecchiette 25
  - Lasagna 99
  - Mozzarella in Carrozza 47
  - Pan Seared Scallops 49
  - Pasta Fagioli 31
  - Penne alla Vodka 107
  - Pork Chops with Cherry Peppers 129
  - Risotto 77

Sicilian Style Stuffed Peppers 53
Spaghetti Carbonara 115
Stuffed Cabbage 83
Stuffed Calamari 155
Stuffed Cherry Peppers 59
Stuffed & Fried Sicilian Olives 57
Stuffed Meatballs 61
Stuffed Mushrooms 63
Stuffed Peppers & Rice 65
Suppli 85
Pepperjack
- Spinach Artichoke Dip 55
Provolone
- Braciole 119
Ricotta
- Aunt Concetta's Manicotti 89
- Eggplant Rollatini 43
- Gnudi 97
- Italian Cheesecake 161
- Lasagna 99
- Lemon Ricotta Cake 167

Chicken
- Chicken Cacciatore 121
- Chicken Meatballs 123
- Chicken Piccata 125
- Easy Whole Roasted Chicken 127
- Stuffed Chicken Cutlets 135
- Stuffed & Fried Sicilian Olives 57

Chicken Broth
- Broccoli Rabe with Sausage & Orecchiette 91
- Creamy Broccoli Soup 21
- Creamy Potato Soup 23
- Escarole & Beans with Sausage & Orecchiette 25
- Lentil Soup 29
- Pasta Fagioli 31

Risotto 77
 Sauteed Cabbage with Pancetta 79
 Sicilian Style Stuffed Peppers 53
 Stuffed Artichokes 81
 Stuffed Calamari 155
 Stuffed Mushrooms 63
Chocolate Chips
 Italian Rainbow Cookies 165
Clams
 Baked Clams 141
 Clam Chowder 17
 Linguine & Clams 101
Cocoa Powder
 Tiramisu 175
Confection Sugar
 Pignoli Cookies 169
Cornmeal, Yellow
 Polenta 73
Crab Meat
 Stuffed Calamari 155
Cream Cheese
 Spinach Artichoke Dip 55
Cream, Heavy
 Asparagus with Béchamel Sauce 71
 Clam Chowder 17
 Cream of Asparagus Soup 19
 Creamy Broccoli Soup 21
 Creamy Potato Soup 23
 Penne alla Vodka 107
 Rice Pudding 171
 Roasted Butternut Squash Soup 33
 Spinach Artichoke Dip 55
Crushed Tomatoes
 Arancini 69
 Pasta alla Norma 105
 Pasta Fagioli 31
 Penne alla Vodka 107

Quick Marinara Sauce 111
Steak Pizzaiola 133
Stuffed Calamari 155
Stuffed Peppers & Rice 65

E

Eggplant
 Eggplant Rollatini 43
 Pasta alla Norma 105
Eggs
 Arancini 69
 Eggplant Rollatini 43
 Fried Burrata Bombs 45
 Gnocchi 95
 Italian Cheesecake 161
 Italian Rainbow Cookies 165
 Lemon Ricotta Cake 167
 Mozzarella in Carrozza 47
 Pork Chops with Cherry Peppers 129
 Rice Pudding 171
 Sicilian Orange Cake 173
 Spaghetti Carbonara 115
 Stuffed & Fried Sicilian Olives 57
 Stuffed Meatballs 61
 Suppli 85
 Tiramisu 175
 Zabaglione 13
Espresso
 Espresso Martini 9
 Tiramisu 175
 Zabaglione 13
Extra Virgin Olive Oil
 Arancini 69
 Asparagus with Béchamel Sauce 71
 Aunt Concetta's Manicotti 89

Braciole 119
Broccoli Rabe with Sausage Orecchiette 91
Bronzino 143
Burrata with Roasted Tomatoes & Garlic 37
Calamari Oreganata 39
Chicken Cacciatore 121
Chicken Meatballs 123
Cod Puttanesca 145
Cream of Asparagus Soup 19
Eggplant Rollatini 43
Escarole & Beans with Sausage & Orecchiette 25
Fried Burrata Bombs 45
Grilled Polpo 147
Insalata di Mare 149
Italian Wedding Soup 27
Lasagna 99
Lentil Soup 29
Linguine & Clams 101
Lobster & Shrimp Fra Diavolo 103
Mozzarella in Carrozza 47
Mussels Marinara 151
Pan Seared Scallops 49
Pasta alla Norma 105
Pasta Fagioli 31
Penne alla Vodka 107
Polenta 73
Pork Chops with Cherry Peppers 129
Red, White and Blue Potatoes 75
Roasted Butternut Squash Soup 33
Sausage with Onions, Fennel & Grapes 131
Shrimp Oreganata 153
Sicilian Style Stuffed Peppers 53

Steak Pizzaiola 133
Stuffed Artichokes 81
Stuffed Calamari 155
Stuffed Cherry Peppers 59
Stuffed Flounder 157
Stuffed & Fried Sicilian Olives 57
Stuffed Meatballs 61
Stuffed Mushrooms 63
Stuffed Peppers & Rice 65
Tripe 137

F

Fennel
  Sausage with Onions, Fennel & Grapes 131
Fish
  Anchovy Fillets
    Calamarata Pasta with Italian Tuna & Tomato Sauce 93
    Cod Puttanesca 145
    Pasta alla Norma 105
    Puttanesca 109
    Sicilian Style Stuffed Peppers 53
    Spaghetti Aglio e Alic 113
    Stuffed Calamari 155
    Stuffed Cherry Peppers 59
  Cod
    Cod Puttanesca 145
  Flounder
    Stuffed Flounder 157
  Tuna
    Calamarata Pasta with Italian Tuna & Tomato Sauce 93
Flour
  Almond Flour
    Sicilian Orange Cake 173

Asparagus with Béchamel Sauce 71
Aunt Concetta's Manicotti 89
Cod Puttanesca 145
Fried Burrata Bombs 45
Gnocchi 95
Gnudi 97
Italian Cheesecake 161
Italian Rainbow Cookies 165
Italian Wedding Soup 27
Lemon Ricotta Cake 167
Lobster & Shrimp Fra Diavolo 103
Mozzarella in Carrozza 47
Sicilian Orange Cake 173
Stuffed & Fried Sicilian Olives 57
Suppli 85

G

Garlic
  Baked Clams 141
  Braciole 119
  Broccoli Rabe with Sausage & Orecchiette 91
  Bronzino 143
  Burrata with Roasted Tomatoes & Garlic 37
  Calamarata Pasta with Italian Tuna & Tomato Sauce 93
  Calamari Oreganata 39
  Chicken Cacciatore 121
  Chicken Meatballs 123
  Chicken Piccata 125
  Clam Chowder 17
  Cod Puttanesca 145
  Cream of Asparagus Soup 19
  Easy Whole Roasted Chicken 127
  Escarole & Beans with Sausage &

Orecchiette 25
Insalata di Mare 149
Italian Wedding Soup 27
Lentil Soup 29
Linguine & Clams 101
Lobster & Shrimp Fra Diavolo 103
Mussels Marinara 151
Pan Seared Scallops 49
Pasta alla Norma 105
Pasta Fagioli 31
Penne alla Vodka 107
Puttanesca 109
Quick Marinara Sauce 111
Roasted Butternut Squash Soup 33
Sausage with Onions, Fennel & Grapes 131
Sauteed Cabbage nwith Pancetta 79
Shrimp Oreganata 153
Sicilian Style Stuffed Peppers 53
Spaghetti Aglio e Alici 113
Steak Pizzaiola 133
Stuffed Artichokes 81
Stuffed Cabbage 83
Stuffed Calamari 155
Stuffed Cherry Peppers 59
Stuffed Flounder 157
Stuffed Meatballs 61
Stuffed Mushrooms 63
Stuffed Peppers & Rice 65
Goat Cheese
  Cream of Asparagus Soup 19
Guanciale
  Spaghetti Carbonara 115

H

Ham
- Eggplant Rollatini 43
- Stuffed Meatballs 61

L

Lemons
- Bronzino 143
- Easy Whole Roasted Chicken 127
- Grilled Polpo 147
- Insalata di Mare 149
- Lemon Ricotta Cake 167
- Limoncello 11
- Red, White and Blue Potatoes 75

Lentils
- Lentil Soup 29

Linguine
- Linguine & Clams 101

M

Marinara Sauce
- Aunt Concetta's Manicotti 89
- Braciole 119
- Chicken Meatballs 123
- Eggplant Rollatini 43
- Gnocchi 95
- Gnudi 97
- Quick Marinara Sauce 111
- Stuffed Cabbage 83
- Tripe 137

Mascarpone
- Tiramisu 175

Milk
- Stuffed Cabbage 83
- Stuffed Meatballs 61

Mozzarella
- Aunt Concetta's Manicotti 89
- Eggplant Rollatini 43
- Mozzarella in Carrozza 47
- Stuffed Meatballs 61
- Suppli 85

Mussels
- Mussels Marinara 151

N

Nutmeg
- Asparagus with Béchamel Sauce 71
- Cream of Asparagus Soup 19
- Creamy Potato Soup 23
- Roasted Butternut Squash Soup 33

Nuts
- Pignoli Nuts
  - Pignoli Cookies 169

O

Octopus
- Grilled Polpo 147

Oil
- Extra Virgin Olive Oil
  - Arancini 69
  - Asparagus with Béchamel Sauce 71
  - Aunt Concetta's Manicotti 89
  - Braciole 119
  - Broccoli Rabe with Sausage & Orecchiette 91
  - Bronzino 143
  - Burrata with Roasted Tomatoes & Garlic 37
  - Calamari Oreganata 39
  - Chicken Cacciatore 121
  - Chicken Meatballs 123
  - Cod Puttanesca 145
  - Cream of Asparagus Soup 19
  - Eggplant Rollatini 43
  - Escarole & Beans with Sausage Orecchiette 25
  - Fried Burrata Bombs 45
  - Grillled Polpo 147
  - Insalata di Mare 149
  - Italian Wedding Soup 27
  - Lentil Soup 29
  - Linguine & Clams 101
  - Lobster & Shrimp Fra Diavolo 103
  - Mozzarella in Carrozza 47
  - Mussel Marinara 151
  - Pan Seared Scallops 49
  - Pasta alla Norma 105
  - Pasta Fagioli 31
  - Penne alla Vodka 107
  - Pork Chops with Cherry Peppers 129
  - Red, White and Blue Potatoes 75
  - Roasted Butternut Squash Soup 33
  - Sausage with Onions, Fennel & Grapes 131
  - Shrimp Oreganata 153
  - Sicilian Style Stuffed Peppers 53
  - Steak Pizzaiola 133
  - Stuffed Artichokes 81
  - Stuffed Calamari 155
  - Stuffed Cherry Peppers 59
  - Stuffed Flounder 157

Stuffed & Fried Sicilian Olives 57
Stuffed Meatballs 61
Stuffed Mushrooms 63
Stuffed Peppers & Rice 65
Tripe 137
Vegetable Oil
- Arancini 69
- Fried Burrata Bombs 45
- Italian Rainbow Cookies 165
- Suppli 85

Olives
- Black Cured Olives
  - Chicken Cacciatore 121
  - Chicken Piccata 125
  - Sicilian Style Stuffed Peppers 53
- Green Olives
  - Calamarata Pasta with Italian Tuna & Tomato Sauce 93
  - Chicken Cacciatore 121
  - Stuffed & Fried Sicilian Olives 57
- Mixed Olives
  - Cod Puttanesca 145
  - Puttanesca 109

Onions
- Baked Clams 141
- Bronzino 143
- Chicken Cacciatore 121
- Chicken Piccata 125
- Cream of Asparagus Soup 19
- Easy Whole Roasted Chicken 127
- Italian Wedding Soup 27
- Penne alla Vodka 107
- Pork Chops with Cherry Peppers 129
- Risotto 77
- Sausage with Onions, Fennel & Grapes 131

Steak Pizzaiola 133

Oranges
- Sicilian Orange Cake 173

Orecchiette
- Broccoli Rabe with Sausage & Orecchiette 91
- Escarole & Beans with Sausage & Orecchiette 25

P

Pancetta
- Sauteed Cabbage with Pancetta 79
- Stuffed Mushrooms 63

Pasta
- Calamarata
  - Calamarata Pasta with Italian Tuna & Tomato Sauce 93
- Ditalini
  - Pasta Fagioli 31
- Lasagna Sheets
  - Lasagna 99
- Orecchiette
  - Broccoli Rabe with Sausage & Orecchiette 91
  - Escarole & Beans with Sausage Orecchiette 25
- Orzo
  - Italian Wedding Soup 27
- Penne
  - Penne alla Vodka 107
- Spaghetti
  - Spaghetti Aglio e Alici 113
  - Spaghetti Carbonara 115

Pecorino Romano
- Arancini 69
- Aunt Concetta's Manicotti 89

Baked Clams 141
Calamari Oreganata 39
Chicken Meatballs 123
Eggplant Rollatini 43
Escarole & Beans with Sausage & Orecchiette 25
Mozzarella in Carrozza 47
Pan Seared Scallops 49
Pasta Fagioli 31
Penne alla Vodka 107
Pork Chops with Cherry Peppers 129
Risotto 77
Sicilian Style Stuffed Peppers 53
Spaghetti Carbonara 115
Stuffed Cabbage 83
Stuffed Calamari 155
Stuffed Cherry Peppers 59
Stuffed & Fried Sicilian Olives 57
Stuffed Meatballs 61
Stuffed Mushrooms 63
Stuffed Peppers & Rice 65
Suppli 85

Pepperjack
- Spinach Artichoke Dip 55

Pepperoncini
- Chicken Cacciatore 121
- Chicken Piccata 125
- Pork Chops with Cherry Peppers 129

Peppers
- Cherry Peppers
  - Pork Chops with Cherry Peppers 129
  - Stuffed Cherry Peppers 59
- Red Peppers
  - Chicken Cacciatore 121

Chicken Piccata 125
 Sicilian Style Stuffed Peppers 53
Roasted Peppers
 Insalata di Mare 149
 Pork Chops with Cherry Peppers 129
Pork
 Italian Wedding Soup 27
 Pork Chops with Cherry Peppers 129
Potatoes
 Bronzino 143
 Chicken Cacciatore 121
 Chicken Piccata 125
 Clam Chowder 17
 Creamy Broccoli Soup 21
 Creamy Potato Soup 23
 Gnocchi 95
 Red, White and Blue Potatoes 75
Prosciutto
 Asparagus with Béchamel Sauce 71
 Braciole 119
 Fried Burrata Bombs 45
 Penne alla Vodka 107
 Scallops Saltimbocca 51
 Stuffed Chicken Cutlets 135
 Stuffed & Fried Sicilian Olives 57
 Stuffed Meatballs 61
Provolone
 Braciole 119

R

Raisins
 Rice Pudding 171
Red Pepper Flakes
 Broccoli Rabe with Sausage &
 Orecchiette 91
Calamarata Pasta with Italian Tuna & Tomato Sauce 93
Cod Puttanesca 145
Escarole & Beans with Sausage Orecchiette 25
Lentil Soup 29
Linguine & Clams 101
Lobster & Shrimp Fra Diavolo 103
Mussels Marinara 151
Pasta alla Norma 105
Pasta Fagioli 31
Penne alla Vodka 107
Puttanesca 109
Quick Marinara Sauce 111
Sauteed Cabbage with Pancetta 79
Sicilian Style Stuffed Peppers 53
Spaghetti Aglio e Alici 113
Steak Pizzaiola 133
Stuffed Calamari 155
Stuffed Peppers & Rice 65
Red Wine
 Chicken Cacciatore 121
 Chicken Piccata 125
 Quick Marinara Sauce 111
 Steak Pizzaiola 133
 Stuffed Calamari 155
 Stuffed Peppers & Rice 65
Rice
 Arborio Rice
  Rice Pudding 171
  Risotto 77
 Risotto Rice
  Risotto 77
 White Rice
  Stuffed Peppers & Rice 65

Ricotta
 Aunt Concetta's Manicotti 89
 Eggplant Rollatini 43
 Gnudi 97
 Italian Cheesecake 161
 Lemon Ricotta Cake 167

S

Sausage
 Broccoli Rabe with Sausage & Orecchiette 91
 Escarole & Beans with Sausage Orecchiette 25
 Sausage with Onions, Fennel & Grapes 131
 Stuffed Cabbage 83
 Stuffed Peppers & Rice 65
Scallops
 Pan Seared Scallops 49
 Scallops Saltimbocca 51
Seafood
 Clams
  Baked Clams 141
  Clam Chowder 17
  Linguine & Clams 101
 Lobster
  Insalta di Mare 149
  Lobster & Shrimp Fra Diavolo 103
 Mussels
  Mussels Marinara 151
 Scallops
  Pan Seared Scallops 49
  Scallops Saltimbocca 51
 Shrimp
  Insalata di Mare 149

Lobster & Shrimp Fra Diavolo 103
Shrimp Oreganata 153

Shallots
Linguine & Clams 101
Pasta Fagioli 31
Roasted Butternut Squash Soup 33
Stuffed Cabbage 83
Stuffed & Fried Sicilian Olives 57

Shrimp
Insalata di Mare 149
Lobster & Shrimp Fra Diavolo 103
Shrimp Oreganata 153

Sour Cream
Creamy Potato Soup 23

Spinach
Gnudi 97
Italian Wedding Soup 27
Spinach Artichoke Dip 55
Stuffed Chicken Cutlets 135

Sugar
Grain Pie 163
Italian Cheesecake 161
Italian Rainbow Cookies 165
Lemon Ricotta Cake 167
Limoncello 11
Penne alla Vodka 107
Pignoli Cookies 169
Rice Pudding 171
Roasted Butternut Squash Soup 33
Sicilian Orange Cake 173
Tiramisu 175
Zabaglione 13

T

Tomatoes
Arancini 69
Bronzino 143
Burrata with Roasted Tomatoes & Garlic 37
Chicken Cacciatore 121
Cod Puttanesca 145
Lobster & Shrimp Fra Diavolo 103
Mussels Marinara 151
Pasta alla Norma 105
Pasta Fagioli 31
Penne alla Vodka 107
Puttanesca 109
Quick Marinara Sauce 111
Steak Pizzaiola 133
Stuffed Calamari 155
Stuffed Peppers & Rice 65

V

Vanilla Extract
Grain Pie 163
Italian Cheesecake 161
Lemon Ricotta Cake 167
Rice Pudding 171
Tiramisu 175

Vegetable Oil
Arancini 69
Fried Burrata Bombs 45
Italian Rainbow Cookies 165
Suppli 85

Vodka
Espresso Martini 9
Limoncello 11
Penne alla Vodka 107

W

White Wine
Baked Clams 141
Clam Chowder 17
Cod Puttanesca 145
Easy Whole Roasted Chicken 127
Linguine & Clams 101
Lobster & Shrimp Fra Diavolo 103
Mussels Marinara 151
Risotto 77
Spaghetti Aglio e Alici 113
Stuffed Calamari 155
Stuffed Flounder 157
Stuffed & Fried Sicilian Olives 57

Z

Zucchini
Lentil Soup 29

Notes & Memories

www.ingramcontent.com/pod-product-compliance
Lightning Source LLC
Chambersburg PA
CBHW041407010526
44107CB00015B/1107